AID, TRADE, AND FARM POLICIES

A SOURCEBOOK ON ISSUES AND INTERRELATIONSHIPS

WINROCK DEVELOPMENT EDUCATION
SERIES

Also in this series

Food, Hunger, and Agricultural Issues:
Proceedings of a colloquium on future U.S. development assistance
Deborah Clubb and Polly C. Ligon, editors

AID, TRADE, AND FARM POLICIES

A SOURCEBOOK ON ISSUES AND INTERRELATIONSHIPS

Proceedings of a workshop
January 4-5, 1989
Washington, D.C.

Edited by
Wayne E. Swegle and Polly C. Ligon

Winrock International Institute for Agricultural Development

December 1989

Workshop sponsored by Winrock International and the U.S. Agency for International Development

Workshop coordinated by Wayne E. Swegle

Sourcebook designed and illustrated by Mike Reagan

Library of Congress Cataloging-in-Publication Data

Aid, trade, and farm policies : a sourcebook on issues and interrelation-
    ships: proceedings of a workshop, January 4-5, 1989, Washington,
    D.C./edited by Wayne E. Swegle and Polly C. Ligon.
            p.   cm.
    December 1989.
    Includes bibliographical references.
    ISBN 0-933595-24-7
    1. Produce trade—Government policy—United States—
Congresses. 2. Agriculture and state—United States—Congresses. 3.
Economic assistance, American-Congresses. 4. United States—Foreign
economic relations—Congresses. I. Swegle, Wayne E. II. Ligon, Polly C.
III. Winrock International Institute for Agricultural Development.
HD9006.A78 1989   89-16729
382'.41'0973—dc20   CIP

AG> Agri

CONTENTS

FOREWORD

Much has been made of the fact that the world is on the verge of a new decade. But the imminence of the 1990s is insignificant unless it is used as a stimulus to make a fresh start by looking for new ways to tackle old problems and conflicts.

For those with a stake in aid, trade, and farm policies, the 1990s will be a crucial time for making a fresh start. The new decade will bring specific opportunities to change and reshape these policies: The 1990 U.S. farm bill, which is being debated, will affect the shape of aid and trade policies. Key trade issues are being discussed in the Uruguay Round of negotiations under the General Agreements on Tariffs and Trade. The outcome will be taken into account in the new farm bill and will affect third world economic development, as well as the competitiveness of U.S. exports.

It is because of these challenges and opportunities that the 1990s are a time for change and not just a change of time.

Part of the tension over aid, trade, and farm policies arises from the wide-ranging goals, needs, perceptions, and viewpoints of farm organizations and development assistance agencies. Both groups have a role in shaping policy and a stake in the outcome of the policy debates. But the interests they represent have often been at odds with each other. One reason for this has been their disparate goals. Another, their failure to communicate these goals to each other.

We at Winrock International felt the need to broaden the dialogue among leaders of farm organizations, congressional committees, and agencies involved in development. Through the Workshop on U.S. Aid, Trade, and Farm Policies: Working Together in the 1990s, and other workshops like it, we have sought to provide a forum for the leaders of these groups to come together and talk honestly and openly; to search for areas of accommodation and agreement; and to devise plans to work together in the coming decade.

This sourcebook records the issues discussed at the workshop and provides direction for those who wish to delve further into the issues. We hope it will promote mutual understanding by all groups with a stake in these issues.

Balancing the needs of U.S. farmers with the need to alleviate poverty and hunger in the third world is a worthy goal. We at Winrock present this sourcebook as a contribution toward achieving this goal.

Robert D. Havener
President
Winrock International Institute for Agricultural Development

PREFACE

This sourcebook presents the results of a 3-day workshop in January 1989 in Washington, D.C., that brought together leaders of farm organizations, congressional committees, and development organizations to discuss the interrelationships between aid, trade, and U.S. farm policy and opportunities for these groups to work together in the 1990s.

The workshop is the third in a series of meetings hosted and coordinated by Winrock International to promote dialogue among various audiences who have interests in and concerns about agricultural development in the third world. Each of these sessions explored a specific aspect of development and U.S. agricultural issues.

The first meeting, held in October 1986 at Winrock's conference center, was cosponsored by the Food and Agriculture Committee of the National Planning Association. Twenty key leaders of development organizations and farm and commodity groups gathered for off-the-record discussions on development assistance and U.S. agricultural issues. The purpose of the meeting was to give these leaders the opportunity to talk face to face in a quiet setting, to look for areas of agreement and disagreement, and to gain a better understanding of each others' positions on development assistance and farm policy.

The second meeting, the "Colloquium on Future U.S. Development Assistance: Food, Hunger, and Agricultural Issues," looked at trends, needs, and issues in international development policy and programs for the 1990s. It was held in February 1988 at Winrock's conference center—one of 11 sessions coordinated by Michigan State University to look at development cooperation in the 1990s. About 35 participants took part in the colloquium, representing development assistance agencies, academic institutions, and private and voluntary organizations. Members of farm and commodity organizations were included, reminding those in the development community of U.S. agriculture's influence on and stake in development assistance programs.

The third workshop brought together leaders of farm and commodity organizations; top staff members of congressional committees that deal with aid, trade, and farm policies; and leaders in the development community. They discussed their points of view on three topics:

- food aid and development assistance to agriculture in the third world
- agricultural aspects of the Uruguay Round of international trade negotiations
- upcoming decisions on future U.S. farm programs

These topics were emphasized because they are interrelated and because legislation and negotiations on all three are under way or forthcoming.

This sourcebook contains the opinion papers written by key leaders in the aid, trade, and farm policy dialogue who addressed the workshop. These papers are supplemented by additional information for those who wish to learn more about the issues.

Three people who do not have papers included in this sourcebook served as session chairs for the workshop and deserve special acknowledgment:

- Duane Acker, assistant to the administrator for food and agriculture at U.S. Agency for International Development
- Clifford M. Hardin, former U.S. Secretary of Agriculture
- Robert Paarlberg, visiting professor of government at Harvard University and associate professor at the Harvard Center for International Affairs

Acker, Hardin, and Paarlberg all have extensive experience in dealing with aid, trade, and farm policies and provided guidance and direction for the workshop discussions.

Special tribute goes to Alan Woods, who served as administrator of the U.S. Agency for International Development (USAID) until his untimely death in June 1989. Mr. Woods was sensitive to U.S. farmers' concerns about agricultural development assistance. As a participant in this workshop, he presented USAID's strategy for the upcoming decade, answered farm organization leaders' and others' questions, and listened to their concerns. Mr. Woods was a vigorous and effective leader for USAID. He is missed.

Wayne E. Swegle
Workshop coordinator and sourcebook editor
Director, Public Affairs and Communication
Winrock International Institute for Agricultural Development

INTRODUCTION

Since the early 1980s, when U.S. farm exports fell and farm incomes declined, farmers and the organizations that represent them have voiced particular concern about the effects of foreign aid policy on their share of the export market. U.S. farmers' concern is a critical political element of the complex mix of aid, trade, and farm policies.

The directions these policies take are influenced by farmers, farm and commodity organizations, politicians, government agencies, and development organizations. A whole range of values, goals, and ideals tangle when the final decisions are made about the course the United States will take concerning aid, trade, and farm policies in the 1990s.

Those with a stake in these policies came to Winrock's January 1989 conference with their own sets of opinions, goals, and needs. At this conference they laid them out on the table and looked for ways to make the policies work effectively for everyone.

IMPORTANCE OF AID POLICIES

One of the major problems in any discussion of aid, trade, and farm policy issues is the fact that they are interrelated and complicated. For many people, aid is the most controversial area and the least understood. That's why it is important to understand what aid is, why it's done, who sets policies, and what agencies carry out the programs. From that point, it is then easier to understand the interrelationships between aid policy and farm and trade policies, and understand the impact of these policies on the United States.

What is aid?

As used here, the term *aid* refers to the assistance provided to about 70 developing countries to help their economies grow so that the quality of peoples' lives is improved. *Developing* countries are those countries that have low per-capita gross national products. Most of these countries are in Latin America, Asia, Africa, and the Middle East.

Aid takes many forms. One type is giving food, medical supplies, or other kinds of material goods needed when natural disasters or famines occur. Another type is making loans or grants to help build roads, schools, or hospitals. Aid can mean sending experts to solve problems or to train others to solve problems.

The types of aid that most directly affect U.S. farmers:

Food aid to developing nations moves through a multitude of U.S. and international assistance programs sponsored by the government, by private organizations, or a combination of both.

P.L. 480 is an example of a U.S. food aid program. It has three titles: Title I concessional sales allow developing countries to buy U.S. farm products at low interest rates with payments stretched for up to 40 years; Title II donation program gives direct food donations to less fortunate people overseas; Title III is designed to help the world's needy people help themselves—it allows governments to buy U.S. agricultural commodities and use them to pay people for self-help programs such as improving storage, transportation, and distribution of farm products.

Agricultural development assistance helps developing countries improve their farm productivity and carries major economic ramifications for American farmers. Continued economic development in a poor country brings increased individual purchasing power; and one of the first things poorer people want is a better, more varied diet. Economic development opens the potential for increased purchases of imported foods. Developing countries purchase about 40% of all exported U.S. goods and services.

Why do development assistance?

A next logical question is: Why do development assistance at all? Here are the most-often cited reasons:

- Humanitarian. Most people support the idea of improving living conditions for all people.
- National and international security. Poverty and hunger sometimes create political and social instability. People become frustrated with their situation and lash out at the government and society.
- Market development. Poor people are not able to buy the products from farms and factories in developed countries. If the incomes of people in developing countries increase, they buy more from developed countries and produce goods and services that developed countries need.

Why help develop third world agriculture?

Many farmers ask why the U.S. should lend development assistance to agriculture—why not build steel mills or develop industry instead? Agricultural development assistance is often a major part of development programs because a high percentage of people in the third world live in rural areas and are engaged in agriculture. Development must start where the people are.

Further, agricultural production usually makes up a large percentage of a developing country's gross national production. Thus, agriculture is the natural place to start the process of economic development. Industrial development has failed in many developing countries because rural people are poor and lack the money to purchase the goods produced by industry. So, agricultural improvement is the starting point of most countries' economic development.

Who carries out development programs?

The U.S. Agency for International Development (USAID) administers important U.S. development-assistance programs. But other agencies such as the U.S. Department of Agriculture (USDA), treasury department, state department, commerce department, and the Overseas Private Investment Corporation also get involved. Additionally, a multitude of development-assistance programs are administered by international organizations such as the World Bank, the Food and Agriculture Organization of the UN, and regional organizations such as the Inter-American Development Bank.

AID'S RELATION TO TRADE AND FARM POLICIES

Policies in different realms of government relate to aid policies. Two important realms of influence are international trade policies and the farm programs of the U.S., other developed countries, and developing nations.

Some examples of these interrelationships:

• The U.S. may provide aid to a country, then turn around and limit imports of that country's production; the damage of the trade policy (limiting imports) may be greater than the value of the aid.

- Or the U.S. may provide aid to a developing country whose principal export product, for example, is sugar; the damage caused by our farm program (a low quota on sugar imports from that country) may be greater than the help from aid.
- Conversely, the protectionist trade policies of a developing country such as South Korea (limiting beef imports, as an example) may hurt U.S. farmers.
- The European Community's trade policy (dumping excess farm production in export markets) flows from its farm policy (guaranteeing high support prices) that hurts U.S. farm exports. This results in retaliatory U.S. farm program legislation and export subsidies (the export enhancement program).

Thus aid, trade, and farm policies need to be considered in tandem.

WHERE THESE POLICIES ARE MADE

In the U.S., *aid policies* are largely determined by the Congress through the foreign aid bill, administered by USAID, and influenced by the wide range of government agencies mentioned earlier.

International *trade rules* are negotiated by the U.S. trade representative and negotiators from other countries under the framework of the General Agreement on Tariffs and Trade (GATT). Since 1948 GATT has served as a forum for trade negotiations and comprises a set of rules that help protect concessions (reductions a country makes in its tariff and nontariff import barriers to induce other countries to reciprocate) and promote fairer trade. Ninety-two countries, accounting for four-fifths of world trade, now belong to GATT. The current Uruguay Round is the eighth round of negotiations since the inception of GATT.

The outcome of the Uruguay Round of negotiations must be approved by the Congress to bind the U.S. to the decisions.

The *farm program* also is written by the Congress and is administered by the U.S. Department of Agriculture. Farm legislation contains food aid provisions, such as P.L. 480, that are administered principally by USDA and USAID. These policies are affected by our national security, international trade balance and federal budget, farm productivity, and humanitarian and similar considerations.

EFFECT OF THE INTERRELATIONSHIPS

Every year, at the international level, advances in communication, transportation, and competitiveness bring all nations into a more tightly integrated package. Policy issues once considered domestic now carry international ramifications as well.

Aid, trade, and farm policies are woven together as closely and delicately as a spider's web; tug on one strand and the others bounce. Congress makes an adjustment in one area, and side effects ripple through the other two.

Aid, trade, and farm policies are being and will be deliberated by the Congress, negotiated in trade talks, and considered by farm, development assistance, and other organizations in 1989 and 1990. It is for these reasons that this workshop looked at the interrelated areas of aid, trade, and farm policies.

Winrock workshop participants questioned the short-term effects of aid to developing countries and what form of development assistance, if any, is best. Several questions surfaced again and again in the discussions:

- Does technical assistance to farmers in developing nations help them become export competitors with U.S. farmers?
- Does increased agricultural production in developing nations actually accelerate market demand for imported U.S.-produced foodstuffs by stimulating individual incomes and thereby a demand for better diets?
- Do substantial amounts of food aid to a developing nation hinder that nation's own agricultural development by discouraging local production?
- Are U.S. or European Community food-aid programs primarily humanitarian efforts or farm-policy tools aimed at removing surplus commodities from a glutted world marketplace without violating international trading rules?

It is hoped this sourcebook will offer valuable background for answering these questions and help inform interested citizens about the issues involved.

FARM, TRADE, AND DEVELOPMENT POLICIES: WHAT THEY MEAN FOR FUTURE U.S. EXPORT MARKETS

Robert L. Thompson
Dean of Agriculture, Purdue University

In the past 15 to 20 years, the economic well-being of American agriculture has become increasingly dependent on the vagaries of the world market and on trade policies. The tremendous export boom of the 1970s, the bust of the early eighties, and the beginnings of the export recovery since 1986 have kept American agriculture on a veritable roller coaster.

More and more U.S. farm and commodity organizations are taking greater interest in the internationalization that American agriculture and associated agribusinesses have undergone. Most of their discussions focus on trade policy, but third world economic development should receive equal, if not higher, billing. Development assistance, trade policies, and U.S. farm programs are closely interrelated issues.

ECONOMIC GROWTH AFFECTS WORLD EXPORT MARKETS

The most important variable influencing the potential size of the market for U.S. agricultural exports in the 1990s and the early twenty-first century will be the rate of economic growth in other countries. Historical data indicates that worldwide economic growth and, in particular, increases in personal income can increase demand for the type of products that the United States exports. In developing countries, incomes are so low that increases in poor people's incomes can lead to an expansion in export markets. Therefore, American agriculture has a tremendous interest in successful, broad-based economic growth around the world and particularly in developing countries. How much of that expanded market the United States captures will depend on its internal policies.

1

In the 1970s, Income Growth
Increased Cereal Consumption

During the 1970s the average annual growth in grain *consumption* for countries outside the United States was 34 million metric tons per year. The rate of growth in grain *production* in these countries during that same decade was 24 million metric tons per year. The gap between consumption and production grew at the rate of 10 million tons per year.

The rate of growth of *production* in countries outside the U.S. accelerated modestly from 24 million metric tons per year in the 1970s to 29 million metric tons per year in the early 1980s—an increase of about 5 million metric tons per year in the annual rate of growth in output.

But the big change in the 1980s was in the rate of growth in cereal *consumption* in other countries, which plummeted from 34 million metric tons per year annual rate of growth in the 1970s to 19 million metric tons per year in the early 1980s.

So, in the early 1980s, production in countries outside the United States was growing at 29 million tons per year and consumption was growing at only 19 million metric tons per year. The gap widened at the rate of 10 million tons per year in the 1970s and started narrowing at the rate of 10 million tons per year in the early 1980s.

A lot of people attributed the export growth of the 1970s to population outrunning food production capacity of the world. If that were the correct explanation, the rate of growth in consumption in the 1980s would have continued at a rate similar to the 1970s.

It didn't. It dropped by almost half from 34 to 19 million metric tons per year in the rest of the world. So, a lot of observers misinterpreted what was going on in the 1970s. What was really causing the rapid growth in cereals consumption around the world in the 1970s was not so much the growth in world population. The population was indeed growing in the 1970s, but, more importantly, per capita incomes around the world, particularly in low-income countries, were growing as well.

Population growth certainly is an important factor in the expansion of aggregate food consumption, and there will be a significant increase in the number of mouths to be fed around the world between now and the early decades of the twenty-first century. But a key issue is how well those new mouths are going to eat. There is a much bigger multiplier on the total demand for grain that comes from income growth than from the growth in population alone.

2

Importing countries are not the only ones who feel the effects on market size from changes in consumption. For example, many U.S. farmers have been extremely concerned about the expansion in exports of soybeans from Brazil in the 1980s. Data from the 1970s shows that Brazil experienced a significant takeoff in soybean production and exports early in the 1970s. Toward the end of the 1970s, though, production was continuing to grow, but exports of both beans and soybean meal were actually falling. Why? Brazil's rapid economic growth caused demand for chicken to grow at such a rapid rate that Brazil's annual consumption for soybean meal and soybeans in the late seventies was actually increasing faster than their production was growing. So exports from Brazil dropped in the last 2 years of the 1970s.

There is a much bigger multiplier on the total demand for grain that comes from income growth than from the growth in population alone.

In the early 1980s, exports of soybeans and soybean products from Brazil took off, but not because they were growing more soybeans. What accounts for much of the early 1980s' increase in Brazil's soybean exports is the fact that consumption declined. Brazil imposed a stringent macroeconomic policy to deal with its debt problems that resulted in a 10% decline in per capita income. This reduced people's purchasing power, and their ability to make discretionary purchases, including animal protein. They reverted back to edible beans for a larger fraction of the protein in their diets, and, as broiler production fell, exports of soybean meal from Brazil increased. Again, this increase in Brazil's exports in the early eighties was not because they were producing more soybeans, but because they were consuming significantly less as a result of the reduction in per capita income.

Changes in per capita incomes have an important effect on import potential in countries like Taiwan and Korea, which were our fastest growing export markets in the 1970s. Per capita income also affects the exporting countries that compete with the United States: faster economic development will reduce their competition with the U.S. in the international market.

3

Third World Markets Have the Greatest Growth Potential

As poor people gain more income, one of the first things they attempt to do is upgrade the quality of their diets. To upgrade the quality of their diets they often consume more animal protein which increases the demand for the feed grains and protein meals necessary to produce that animal protein. American farmers benefit since they are among the world's most efficient producers of feed grains and protein meals.

Economic development is concerned with raising per capita incomes. Raising the national average per capita income is not really our concern, because that can be done by raising the income of the top 10% of the income classes by a large fraction and leaving untouched the bottom 90%. That would have little effect on total food consumption. What third world countries really need is economic growth that affects all segments of the population and does not leave the poorest of the poor behind. So, third world development should focus on broad-based economic growth.

It is important to recognize that one of the poorest groups in most third world countries is the rural poor. Certainly there are many urban poor, but the rural poor are among the most numerous of the impoverished groups in third world countries, and they, too, will upgrade the quality of their diets when the opportunity is provided.

National economic development inevitability leads first to a reduction of the percentage of the population employed in agriculture and eventually to a reduction in the absolute number of people employed in agriculture. But if labor is to be released from agriculture to the growing manufacturing and, eventually, service sectors of those economies, an initial increase in agricultural production is essential.

I know of no country that has achieved rapid economic growth or significant growth in per capita income that has not also developed its agriculture along the way. But, in every case that I have examined, the data also shows per capita incomes grow fast enough that the increase in consumption of agricultural products grows much more rapidly than the increase in agricultural production itself.

Few countries have sustained a 3% annual growth in agricultural production over any extended period of time—in fact, 2¹/₂% per year is considered good. On the other hand, when population growth is considered along with the effect of increased per capita incomes in poor countries, it is not at all difficult to see 6% to 7¹/₂% per year annual growth in consumption of agricultural products. It is easy to achieve consumption growth rates that are 4% and

4

even 5% faster than increases in food production in such countries. Therefore, third world countries are good potential growth markets—if they are permitted to export goods in which they have a comparative advantage so they have the foreign exchange to pay for their imports.

U.S. Policy Affects U.S. Market Share

To expand the total size of the market, the single most important factor will be the rate of economic growth, particularly in the third world. But, the U.S. share of third world markets depends upon U.S. policies. In the 1970s the United States captured virtually all the 10 million-ton-per-year annual growth in world grain trade because it was highly competitive. Loan rates were down to competitive levels in the late 1960s, the dollar was devalued twice in the early 1970s, and about 60 million acres of land had been set aside through the old soil bank and related programs. So the United States could rapidly expand supply and was in a highly competitive price position that permitted it to capture most of the growth in the world market.

In 1981, a number of factors developed that changed the world from the situation of the 1970s. The 1981 farm bill legislated rigid minimum loan rates and in effect, announced to the world the minimum prices the United States would take for our exports for the next 4 years. Thus, the United States invited its competitors to underprice it by just enough to take away export markets.

On top of that, the United States imposed rigorous macroeconomic policies to break the back of double-digit inflation. But these stringent macroeconomic policies created such confidence in the American economy that the price of the dollar (the exchange rate) was bid up by about half. When combined with the rigid minimum-loan rates, this made it virtually impossible for the United States to compete in the world market, and U.S. farm exports fell by 40% in 5 years.

Furthermore, as the total size of the world market shrank, increased competition created an environment that was propitious for protectionism to raise its ugly head around the world.

The Food Security Act of 1985 fixed one of the important problems in the 1981 farm bill. The 1985 farm bill provided downward flexibility in loan rates, and it also authorized a number of other measures, including the export enhancement program, to facilitate recovery of export markets that had been taken away through unfair competition—particularly through export subsidies from the Common Market. The dollar also has come down by a substantial margin. Together, these measures have put the United States back in a competitive position in world markets.

5

THE UNITED STATES CAN GAIN FROM LIBERALIZED TRADE

In the future, our ability to compete for a share of the world market will be determined, not only by our own policies, but by world agricultural trade policies as well.

In the current round of international trade negotiations, agriculture is high on the agenda. Much of what we have heard to date about the Uruguay Round, and how essential it is for all countries to make progress in liberalizing international markets, has been oriented towards reducing subsidies and protectionist devices that hamper U.S. exports and gaining greater market access for U.S. exports overseas. This is extremely important because American agriculture has everything to gain from allowing comparative advantage to work and from opening up markets.

Trade Barriers Will Probably be Reduced, Not Eliminated

If we are to expect to achieve cuts in subsidies and in protectionism around the world, the United States will have to put its own protectionist barriers on the negotiating table. I think that there is sufficient worldwide concern about protectionism that by the time the Uruguay Round is over, some headway will have been made toward reducing farm subsidies and protectionist devices which distort trade and interfere with the working of comparative advantage. It is not likely that all agricultural subsidies around the world will be eliminated in the next decade. But, a significant across-the-board reduction in agricultural subsidies could be achieved in this GATT round. Then, in 5 years or so, more cuts can be made.

In manufacturing trade, progress was made toward liberalization by cutting tariffs across-the-board on all products in all countries simultaneously, instead of by the offers and requests approach used in earlier GATT rounds. In ensuing GATT rounds, tariffs were reduced by 20% or 30% over 5 years or so. Today there are only very modest tariff barriers to international trade in manufactured goods.

In agriculture, little progress has been made toward trade liberalization because agricultural policies have never been on the bargaining table. Now, domestic policies are fair game, and if across-the-board cuts in all commodities in all countries simultaneously are insisted upon, I feel some progress toward liberalizing agricultural trade can be made.

Third World Countries Will Benefit From Freer Trade

An important benefit of freer and more-open world trading environment is often omitted from discussions. Third world countries, which are our greatest potential growth markets for farm products in which we have a comparative advantage, will benefit significantly from a freer and more open trading environment. Countries like Korea and Taiwan, which are often held up as examples of successful economic development, have been some of our best growth markets. Those countries succeeded because they underwent export-led economic development. One of the more important factors in their successful development was that they did not follow a protectionist, import-substitution path of economic development. Rather, they identified industries in which they had comparative advantage and permitted them to trade and to grow, free of as many distortions as possible. Those industries thrived and national economic development proceeded at relatively rapid rates. And American agriculture benefited from that growth.

So, a freer and more open trading environment would certainly be of value, not only to American agriculture but also to the economic growth of those markets to which we hope to sell more products in the 1990s and the early twenty-first century.

AID TO DEVELOPING COUNTRIES CAN BENEFIT U.S. FARMERS

Many observers are concerned that food aid gluts developing countries' markets, drives down market prices, and destroys the incentive to local farmers, thus setting back agricultural development. This happens in many third world countries where agriculture already is a disadvantaged sector. Historically, most developing countries have taxed, not subsidized, their agricultural sectors. Agriculture has already suffered from enough barriers to development in such countries. The last thing they need is for a lot of food aid to get dumped into the market and further reduce incentives to development.

On the other hand, there is evidence that food aid, when judiciously utilized, can be an important resource transfer from high-income to low-income countries. Food-for-work programs are one example. In this type of project, people who do not have the money to buy food are employed productively in development projects and paid with food. The market demand for food is not

7

reduced because these people did not have the money to purchase the food from the market in the first place. By such in-kind transfers of food, effective investments in development projects are achieved and the real incomes of poor people are increased. The Food for Progress program, put in place several years ago, has demonstrated that there are opportunities for more-effectively utilizing surplus stocks as a means of transferring resources from high-income countries to poor third world countries.

American Farmers Can Benefit
From Imported Genetic Materials

American agriculture has a tremendous opportunity to benefit from genetic materials collected in third world countries in exchange for the basic research techniques the United States shares with the third world.

American agriculture has a tremendous opportunity to benefit from genetic materials collected in third world countries in exchange for the basic research techniques the United States shares with the third world.

Some foreign countries are so concerned about the value of their genetic material that they are hesitant about letting U.S. scientists onto their research stations for fear of losing a favored market position. My point is that here again is an area where there is a lot of misinformation. Many people incorrectly feel that we have all the technological answers in the United States. Again, I feel, as a dean of a land-grant college of agriculture, U.S. farmers benefit significantly from the flow of technology that comes back to the states from countries in which the United States may be involved in developing an agricultural research capacity or a college of agriculture.

Land-grant universities and other American agricultural research institutions have been criticized by commodity organizations for giving away our agricultural technology and, in turn, our comparative advantage through agricultural development projects. Certainly technological change is an important shifter of comparative advantage in agriculture around the world. But commodity organizations fail to appreciate the importance of the two-way transfer of technology that goes on when land-grant universities and other American research institutions are involved in agricultural projects in third world countries.

For example, all the genetic material resistant to rust now in American wheat varieties has come from Africa. Previously no American varieties were resistant to rust. Sorghum, one of the important drought-tolerant crops in the semiarid parts of the United States, was developed in East Africa. It may have genes that could be spliced into corn, using genetic engineering techniques, to give corn greater drought tolerance.

U.S. AGRICULTURE NEEDS THIRD WORLD MARKETS

The topics addressed in this paper—development assistance, trade policy, and farm programs—are deeply interwoven and have strong international components. To have a profitable and economically healthy American agriculture in the 1990s and the early twenty-first century of a similar size to that which exists today, export performance must be maintained. If farm sector and associated agribusinesses are to grow, or presently underutilized resources put back to work, the United States will have to export more because overseas markets are the only markets with growth potential. This means competing under the same rules as our trading partners and removing policy barriers that interfere with moving U.S. commodities in the world market.

The United States must not let its own policies—whether they be farm policies that set price supports too high or macroeconomic policies that cause the dollar to be overvalued—artificially price its products out of the market.

U.S. AGRICULTURE'S STAKE IN AID AND TRADE

Kenneth L. Bader
Chief Executive Officer, American Soybean Association

A few years ago the American Soybean Association (ASA) and other farm and commodity groups began to openly question some of the programs carried out abroad by the U.S. Agency for International Development (USAID) and other development institutions. Since these questions were raised, I have been asked at least four or five times to address the issue of the relationship between U.S. agriculture and foreign assistance. There has been a continuing—and often conflicting—dialogue on the relationship between agriculture and development. This dialogue is leading to a better understanding of the issues by American farmers and the development community.

U.S. FARMERS' NEEDS SHOULD TAKE PRIORITY

American farmers understand that future growth in exports will come from the scores of developing nations that are slowly climbing up the economic ladder. Those of us in the soybean industry know that economic growth is necessary if developing nations are to increase their consumption of vegetable oils and begin developing demand for the meat, milk, and eggs that are produced with soybean meal. We also realize that foreign assistance can and should play an important role in expediting needed economic growth in developing nations.

However, U.S. foreign assistance activities and programs should be designed and administered in such a way that they enhance the opportunity for future export growth for U.S. soybean farmers. Specific changes that will help expand export markets include reorganizing the administration of food aid programs, directing development assistance toward the private sector, making third world debt reduction a priority in development programs, and phasing out trade-distorting subsidies.

Blind faith in the benefits of foreign assistance and overseas economic development is not good enough. U.S. farmers need more assurance that what is good for the nations the United States assists is also good for the U.S. economy.

Food Aid Allocation and Administration Should be Changed

Many U.S. farm organizations are concerned with the way food assistance programs are administered. Currently, recipients of Title I loans under the Food for Peace program (Public Law 480) have no assurance they will be allocated loans in the next fiscal year. And they are never sure when they will reach agreement with the U.S. on terms for the loans. This on-again, off-again approach interferes with orderly delivery of commodities to the recipient countries and is detrimental to U.S. suppliers and the recipient nations alike.

Blind faith in the benefits of foreign assistance and overseas economic development is not good enough. U.S. farmers need more assurance that what is good for the nations the United States assists is also good for the U.S. economy.

Members of U.S. farm organizations, like many in the humanitarian community, also have concerns with the way U.S. food assistance programs are allocated among nations. It takes only a cursory look at the Public Law 480 recipient list for fiscal year 1989 to see that needs of recipient nations are secondary to national security and foreign policy when it comes to deciding who gets funds and the amount they receive. It appears that more and more, our food assistance programs are being used as debt rescheduling mechanisms rather than to achieve the objectives for which they were designed.

In the past, ASA and other agricultural organizations have not spoken in a single coordinated voice to express our concerns and recommendations to the executive branch and the U.S. Congress. But now ASA and several other agricultural and commodity organizations have joined together to establish the Committee on Agricultural Trade and Foreign Assistance. This ad hoc committee is formulating a common policy on several issues. The committee will soon release its first policy paper supporting changes in the Public Law 480 program to maximize its effectiveness. The paper will be widely distributed within the new administration and the Congress. Additional papers will be issued as we formulate our

12

positions on various issues. Our goal is to be a major player in reviewing and revamping our nation's overall food assistance and development programs.

The last group that studied U.S. export trade policies was the National Commission on Agricultural Trade and Export Policy. The commission was composed of representatives of Congress, the administration, and the private sector. It issued its final report on July 1, 1986. With respect to reorientation of food aid and economic assistance, the commission's report recommended that

- explicit requirements be put into effect to insure that food aid and foreign economic assistance programs serve U.S. agricultural market development interests
- the Secretary of Agriculture be assigned a greater leadership role in food aid and foreign economic assistance matters
- all food aid programs currently authorized by law be fully used to export U.S. surpluses
- safeguards be put in place to ensure that U.S. agricultural assistance programs do not run counter to U.S. agricultural trade interests

Development Assistance Should Go to the Private Sector

Those in agriculture will agree that private sector capitalism is the engine that will bring about economic growth in developing nations. When I refer to the private sector I mean businesses that depend on a profit for their survival. All of our development programs should be aimed at helping the private sector in developing nations. We should avoid programs that concentrate more power and resources in the hands of governments. One need look no farther than the economic miracles of Korea, Taiwan, and Malaysia to know that the best means of improving the lives of people in developing nations is through the private sector.

The operation of our foreign assistance programs can be improved in several ways. First, we should develop long-term plans aimed at systematically moving nations up the economic ladder. For example, one goal should be to gradually reduce the level of subsidy provided to poor nations. To accomplish this goal, Public Law 480 loans can be started at low interest rates and gradually increased as the nation's economy improves. As much as possible the local currency reflows should be used to build needed infrastructure to receive, store, transport, and utilize food and feed commodities. Over time we should move the nations off of Public Law 480 and onto the intermediate-term credit program with commercial interest rates on 10-year loans. Finally, the country should be moved onto the short-term credit program and commercial sales.

It may not be enough to simply remodel the current foreign assistance delivery system. It may be more practical to abolish USAID, the Overseas Private Investment Corporation, the Office of International Cooperation and Development, and other agencies if they are not performing the functions mandated by law, and start over. Our programs should not be reshaped to meet our delivery mechanism. Rather, a delivery mechanism must be built to meet today's and tomorrow's needs. Possibly humanitarian assistance should be delineated from economic and trade development. A new agency could be established to carry out bona fide humanitarian assistance while another would carry out economic and trade development. Each agency would have a clearly defined mission. Thus, humanitarian assistance could be provided when needed and economic development when practical.

Reducing Third World Debt is a Priority

Humanitarian assistance and development as part of the solution to the third world debt crisis should be considered. Recognition that major debtor nations like Mexico and Brazil are not going to be able to repay their foreign debts is growing. As long as the debts remain, the debtor nations are going to have to maintain tough austerity programs, which will stifle development, foster malnutrition, and undermine their already weak democracies. A debt reduction program is the only way to help the debtor nations recover.

Debt reduction should not be without restrictions. Debtor nations should be directed to use their foreign exchange savings to feed their people better, foster private sector development, and improve the education of their children. This action will transform foreign debt into developmental assets and will help developing nations afford commodity imports to meet their food and development needs. I know of no other way to quickly boost world economic growth to the benefit of all nations.

It is extremely important that public interests are taken into account when a debt reduction program is implemented. Otherwise, the benefits will accrue solely to the financial community.

Subsidies Distort Market Signals
and Hurt Developing Countries

Trade policy must also play a key role in building the economies of developing nations. ASA believes the U.S. government's GATT proposal for a 10-year phaseout of all trade-distorting agricultural subsidies is the best course to pursue. Nothing hurts farmers in developing countries more than the enormous subsidies developed countries give their own farmers.

The European Community alone provides an estimated $100 billion in direct and indirect subsidies to its farmers while closing its markets to imports of many products produced by developing nations. By phasing out these subsidies, comparative advantage will rule world trade rather than government distortions. This phase-out must apply to developing as well as developed nations.

The United States simply cannot afford to ignore its own problems if it is to maintain its economic security and way of life. U.S. trade and foreign assistance programs must serve U.S. citizens first and other nations second.

A major reason for the poor performance of agriculture in developing nations is that market signals are distorted by the governments of those nations. Price controls on basic foodstuffs in many nations have taken away all incentives for farmers to produce. The distortions must be removed.

THE UNITED STATES CANNOT IGNORE ITS OWN ECONOMIC PROBLEMS

Times have changed in the world economy and we must accept those changes. Twenty years ago the United States had not only the strongest economy in the world, but also was the largest lender nation on earth. U.S. products were competitive all around the world. The United States could afford to allocate many of its resources to assist other countries with their development.

Today the United States is the world's largest debtor nation and has enormous trade and budget deficits. Many U.S. products are no longer competitive in the international market. The United States simply cannot afford to ignore its own problems if it is to maintain its economic security and way of life. U.S. trade and foreign assistance programs must serve U.S. citizens first and other nations second.

TRADE AND AID POLICIES: HOW U.S. FARMERS SEE IT

Dean Kleckner
President, American Farm Bureau Federation

I'd like to provide my version of a farmer's view of U.S. aid and trade policies within the complicated context of the new administration, the new developments at the General Agreement on Tariffs and Trade (GATT) negotiations, and the new farm program.

HOW FARMERS VIEW TRADE

In the 1988 elections, farm voters across the nation did not support the more-strident protectionist candidates, or the candidates who called for more federal involvement in farm programs. These candidates were rejected by farm voters in about the same proportion as they were rejected by all voters. This and other examples are clues to farmers' views on trade issues. In general, farmers want a more liberalized trade policy and are concerned with unfair trade practices.

Farmers Lean Toward Open Trade Policy

Farm and ranch people generally backed the 1988 trade bill passed by Congress—legislation that moved away from protectionism and toward freer, more-open international trade. Many members of Congress specifically opposed the highly protectionist Gephardt amendment that, for a time, was included in the trade bill. This amendment would have required bilateral negotiations with any country that maintained what was termed "a pattern of unjustifiable trade policies," or, had unjustifiable trade surpluses with the United States. Of course, the term *unjustifiable* was wide-open to interpretation.

Under the proposed amendment, these bilateral trade negotiations were to be aimed at reducing the trade surpluses by 10% per year. Should negotiations on how to do this fail, the Gephardt amendment would have required across-the-board retaliation against all products exported to the United States by the offending

17

·

countries until the prescribed 10% reduction in the trade deficit was reached. For the first year after negotiations, the revised amendment would have required the president to retaliate only against specific imports being traded unfairly, rather than against all imports as in the earlier version. However, after that first year, U.S. retaliation would be across-the-board just as called for in the original amendment.

While farmers joined Congress in turning thumbs down on the Gephardt amendment, they supported a number of positive provisions offered in last year's trade bill legislation. These included an increase in funds and personnel for the U.S. Department of Agriculture's Foreign Agricultural Service, and creation of agricultural aid-and-trade missions designed to coordinate U.S. food-aid and trade-policy goals in cooperation with the private sector.

Farmers generally support strong U.S. responses to foreign unfair trade practices. They opposed the Gephardt amendment primarily because it was aimed at curbing the level of imports rather than attacking specific unfair trade practices.

Unfair Trade Practices are a Key Concern

To farmers, fairness is often a key issue. Unfair trade practices take many forms and the reasons given for them often are rationalized using convoluted logic. For example, for a number of years, U.S. fear of foot-and-mouth disease in European cattle—and our import prohibitions caused by it—has been looked upon by the Europeans as little more than a veterinarian-imposed trade barrier. After all, they have learned to live with the disease and think the United States could too. To an American cattleman, this is almost insanely illogical. The United States probably will continue to go to great lengths to keep from importing cattle with foot-and-mouth disease.

In recent months, the Europeans hit on the idea of a livestock growth hormone ban to keep U.S. meat out of their markets, citing possible health risks that had been mentioned by some of their consumer groups. Under the ban, no U.S. meat suspected of being produced with growth hormones can enter any of the 12 countries in the European Common Market. Such actions are commonly called nontariff trade barriers. The United States responded by imposing a 100% tariff on $100 million worth of European foods. The $100 million represents the value of the banned U.S. meat.

The United States could retaliate in yet another way. A provision of the 1988 U.S. trade bill, which U.S. farmers supported, allows the United States to ban meat imported from any country with inspection systems that are less-sophisticated than those of the United States. But, retaliation produces retaliation. The Meat Export Federation indicates there are at least four tiers of possible retaliation in the current meat battles. Before long we could be engaged in a full-scale trade war with one of our allies and best customers. However, GATT has the potential to help us solve such problems.

HOW FARMERS VIEW AID

The confusion and worry that farmers feel about foreign aid is reflected in policy proposals written for consideration by Farm Bureau's House of Delegates at its 1989 annual meeting.

In preparing for this meeting, the resolutions committee of the Farm Bureau, which is composed of all the state Farm Bureau presidents, met in mid-December 1988. They reviewed dozens of proposed resolutions from farmers all over the country, including those dealing with national farm programs, international trade, and international aid. The Farm Bureau's policy statement is reached through a year-long process that reflects the core of farm and ranch thinking.

The farmers' input shows that they have become quite sensitized to aid and its relationship to U.S. trade. Farmers are generally skeptical about technical aid, but feel that existing food aid programs, such as the Food for Peace program, and alternate approaches to food aid, such as a world food fund, can be beneficial. However, farmers also feel that food aid cannot create stability in politically unstable countries.

Technical Aid that Helps Competitors Should be Stopped

While it may be completely obvious to some people that national development and improved buying power of lesser-developed countries is closely tied to agricultural development, farmers have real difficulty in seeing it this way. Most U.S. farmers cannot understand—or don't want to understand—why we should give away our research and resulting technology. Why should we voluntarily finance, train, and equip our own competition for world markets?

While it is possible to demonstrate how helping the agriculture of a less-developed country eventually brings more buying power and generates new farm markets, most farmers won't buy it. The prospect of improved third world markets in the future is

19

small compensation or incentive for today's farmer in the United States who may feel that he is living on the ragged edge of financial disaster and probably won't be around long enough to benefit from foreign aid. This cynicism is reflected in the Farm Bureau's policy statement opposing technical aid:

We oppose economic and(or) technological aid through any state, federal, or international program which contributes to the production or distribution of any agricultural products by our foreign competitors which adversely affect the interests of U.S. producers. Assistance currently in place should be curtailed immediately.

Food for Peace is the Right Kind of Approach

The Food for Peace program (Public Law 480) is a clear-cut example of an aid program that serves a wide variety of interests, including farmers' interests. Even though the primary objective of the program is to meet humanitarian needs, Public Law 480 also serves foreign policy, national security, surplus control, and market development needs.

Farm Bureau helped originate Public Law 480, a concept first developed in a community Farm Bureau discussion and then endorsed by the county, state, and American Farm Bureaus. Farm Bureau's new policy recommends that the program be expanded, particularly in areas of the world that are suffering from drought or locusts, or are otherwise plagued by hunger problems.

Food Is Not the Answer to Political Instability

Farmers believe that food aid cannot solve the problems of countries that are politically unstable. In many countries, warring leaders use food as a weapon against their own citizens. Those who control the roads, the treasury, or the food, control the people. Even the U.S. government has tried to use food as a diplomatic weapon from time to time by imposing embargoes.

An electric fence stretches across the border between starving Mozambique and food-plentiful South Africa. Once a food exporter, Mozambique now produces something less than 10% of its food needs. Reeling from hunger and violence and, despite the killer fence, a half million Mozambicans have fled the country and their own leftist leaders.

Burma was one of Asia's potentially richest nations before more than 25 years of a totalitarian, centrally directed economy turned it into one of the world's poorest countries. Its economy is in shambles and its people in riot. Reports show that thousands of citizens have been killed by an authoritarian regime trying to hold power in the face of nation-wide protest.

The secret, of course, is to break the cycle and get these economies moving again. Until that occurs, aid can do little other than buy time. Productive agriculture requires a stable, cooperative government, not raging civil war.

The prospect of improved third world markets in the future is small compensation for today's farmer in the U.S. who may feel that he is living on the ragged edge of financial disaster and probably won't be around long enough to benefit from foreign aid.

Former U.S. Secretary of Agriculture, Ezra Taft Benson, made this plain years ago when he noted that abundance is not possible without incentive—and that freedom to receive rewards from one's labors is the most sustaining incentive of all. The profit motive, said Benson, diminishes in proportion to the increase in government controls, regulations, and taxes.

A WORLD FOOD FUND
IS AN ALTERNATIVE FORM OF AID

Perhaps we should remember from time to time how drought, floods, locusts, and other natural disasters have greatly diminished world food supplies. Edouard Saouma, head of the Food and Agricultural Organization of the United Nations, recently gave a gloomy report listing all of the physical reasons for the diminishing food reserves. But equal attention should be paid to the political reasons that are far more devastating to food supplies in developing countries.

The lack of money, not shortages of commodities in world markets, is the limiting factor in food aid programs. Farm Bureau continues to call for donations to an international fund to buy food commodities to meet emergency food needs. When the situation allows, participating nations would be permitted to give part of their contribution in commodities rather than currency. Even the poorest of nations could contribute according to ability.

It is interesting to note that Farm Bureau has been suggesting this solution for about 30 years without any other private or public agency, organization, church denomination, or social-action group accepting the challenge, or for that matter, showing the least bit of interest in a world food fund. Farm Bureau will continue to offer this idea and continue to work in the vast fields of international trade and aid.

WHAT FARMERS THINK CAN INFLUENCE POLICY

Historian Barbara Tuchman once said that "bystanders have no history of their own." She said that while they are on stage and may even see things that go unnoticed by the actors and the audience, bystanders have no effect and no part in the action. "They are not even the audience," she observed.

Farmers and ranchers are not bystanders. They know they are on stage; they know they sometimes see opportunities and reach conclusions that others do not. They will continue to be active players in the field of trade and aid, knowing that the results of what they think and do can influence the world.

USAID AND U.S. FARMERS: COMMON GOALS AND CONCERNS

Alan Woods
Administrator, U.S. Agency for International Development

Today—more than ever before—it is clear that the development community and the U.S. agricultural community share common interests. The evidence rolling in shows that

- Economic growth in developing nations is increasing family incomes, purchasing power, and employment.
- This increase in prosperity is leading to increased consumption, particularly the consumption of food.
- A significant portion of that increase in food consumption is from new demand for imported foods.
- Increased demand for imported food is good news to U.S. farmers who export that food.

Everybody benefits from progress in developing countries. Economic success for developing countries means economic success for American farmers. Thus, while the primary task of the U.S. Agency for International Development (USAID) is to help developing countries attain sustainable, long-term economic development and U.S. agriculture's focus is on its own future, there are compelling reasons for these two groups to share ideas.

USAID wants farmers' views on

- how USAID can be most effective in carrying out its mission
- how USAID can operate to ensure that our development efforts—and those of other donors—will be helpful, not harmful, to U.S. agriculture

USAID'S PROGRAMS HELP U.S. FARMERS AND DEVELOPING COUNTRIES

USAID has produced a report on future USAID programs and policies for food and agriculture (see appendix 3).

Here are some of the conclusions we reached in this report.

1. A priority USAID task is to increase the incomes of the poor in developing countries. Our experience has shown that where

higher incomes are generated, they translate into better diets, health care, and education, and more-productive investments. Higher incomes don't happen magically. They are a contributor to and a result of broad-based economic growth. So, when USAID says higher incomes are a priority, it means it is committed to strategies that foster overall economic growth in the developing countries.

2. Increased food availability and consumption improves people's physical and mental productivity. Increased productivity triggers economic growth that leads to higher incomes.
3. Once basic caloric needs are met and productivity and incomes begin to increase, the demand for vegetables, meats, and processed foods increases. As this demand increases, a new round of production is triggered, generating a new wave of entrepreneurial and employment opportunities. The benefits spread in an ever-widening circle.
4. The economic policies and regulations that countries embrace have a tremendous influence on their growth. Experience has shown that market-oriented economic policies have the best track record when it comes to promoting growth. So, those are the kinds of policies USAID promotes.

The conclusions from this report provide a basis for USAID programs that serve U.S. farmers' need for export markets and developing countries' needs for economic growth and food.

Economic Development Builds Markets

For U.S. agriculture and rural America to thrive, export markets need to expand. The export markets with the greatest potential for expansion lie in developing countries.

The majority of the world's population lives in developing countries. For the foreseeable future that majority will increase. Population growth rates in these countries are slowing but they still outpace those of developed countries. If people in developing countries could afford it, they would already be the fastest growing consumers of food. In contrast, in Western Europe, Japan, and other developed countries, per capita food consumption has plateaued as nutritional needs have been satisfied and population growth rates have slowed.

The relationship between economic growth and rising food demand has been confirmed by recent research conducted by the U.S. Department of Agriculture (USDA). USDA's work shows that in developing countries where significant economic growth has occurred, the demand for food—more and higher-quality food—

has increased sharply. Further, in situations where family incomes are rising and population growth remains high, the demand for food can exceed what a country's expanding agricultural system can supply. That's why the economically expanding developing countries have become potential markets for U.S. agriculture.

For U.S. agriculture and rural America to thrive, export markets need to expand. The export markets with the greatest potential for expansion lie in developing countries.

Where economic growth is rapid, the potential for U.S. agricultural sales is strong, and growing stronger. Both U.S. farmers and people in developing countries benefit from these sales.

Food Aid Creates Markets for U.S. Products

People in developing countries also benefit from America's ability to produce agricultural surpluses and to transform those surpluses into food aid. Through food aid programs, hungry people are fed and developing nations are introduced to U.S. products. Once introduced, they tend to stay acquainted.

Many of the best customers for U.S. agricultural exports have been food aid recipients at one time or another. For example, South Korea now buys more food in one year than the United States gave that nation in all the years it sent food aid. And food aid—when used carefully—has a unique value: sometimes it can stimulate development where cash cannot.

LIBERALIZED TRADE SERVES U.S. AND DEVELOPING COUNTRY INTERESTS

USAID and the U.S. agricultural community have a lot in common and these two groups are beginning to understand the extent of their mutual interests. The agricultural community in the United States and the agricultural communities in developing countries also have mutual interests that need to be more fully articulated and better understood. For example, both communities have a lot to gain from achieving their goals for agriculture through the General Agreement on Tariffs and Trade (GATT), which is currently in another round of negotiations.

If liberalization in agricultural trade can be achieved through the GATT negotiations, both the United States and developing countries will benefit. In a liberalized trading environment, developing countries that pursue a policy of self-reliance in agriculture will tend to produce and export what they can produce efficiently. They will import products they cannot grow efficiently. The United States and other developed nations will do the same and the markets for agricultural products the United States produces efficiently will expand rather than contract.

Ideally, USAID can create a lot of "win-win"
situations—where developing countries and
U.S. agriculture both benefit.

With a reduction in subsidies and protectionism by both the U.S. and competing countries, the United States can be very competitive in world agricultural markets. Greater liberalization in agricultural trade is not only desirable, it's absolutely necessary for both the United States and the developing countries.

FARMERS AND USAID
MUST WORK TOGETHER

This is a time of change. The world economy has undergone an extensive transformation in the past 20 years. The U.S. economy—including the U.S. agricultural economy—is more dependent than ever on international trade.

In recent years world capital markets have become highly integrated and free-floating exchange rates have led to large swings in exchange and interest rates. U.S. farmers are only too familiar with, for example, how an overvalued dollar can reduce U.S. farm exports.

Thus, in a number of ways, the well-being of the United States is becoming dependent on the well-being of the rest of the world. This interdependence will increase as we move into the twenty-first century.

Now, in this time of transition, it's worth thinking about where the United States is going. Over the past 8 years, the Reagan administration set in motion a revolution in the way government does business. There is every reason to expect that the momentum of that effort will be maintained by the Bush administration.

Certainly that will be the case for U.S. farm policy. The farm bill probably will be refined in 1990, saving, of course, the good features of the 1985 bill. Today's farm bill not only legislates all farm income and price support programs but also our food aid policy. In that context, it is worth noting that there is a good chance that the foreign assistance bill will also be rewritten in the near future.

That's why those concerned with USAID's policies need to take the time to explore new food aid approaches as well as other steps to foster the economic growth that is so important for the future of developing countries.

USAID's food and agriculture directions in the 1990s will have a major impact on the speed and sustainability of economic progress in the developing countries. In turn, total development efforts, including food aid, will have an important effect on the long-term export potential of the U.S. agriculture community.

Ideally, USAID can create a lot of "win-win" situations— where developing countries and U.S. agriculture both benefit. The future size of the U.S. agricultural export market is intimately tied to USAID's success in increasing developing country incomes. In that light, it is very much in the interest of the U.S. agricultural community to make sure USAID does its job well— and that it has the tools to do it.

THE ROLE OF THE WORLD BANK IN THE DEBATE ON AID, TRADE, AND AGRICULTURAL POLICIES

Michel Petit
Director, Agriculture and Rural Development
The World Bank

U.S. policies and economic phenomena affecting the country's position on aid, international trade, and domestic farm issues are closely interrelated. Public awareness of these interrelationships has placed the World Bank in a visible and, therefore, quite vulnerable position with respect to the domestic U.S. policy debate. This was illustrated recently when approval of the U.S. contribution to the capital increase of the World Bank—already agreed to by its board of executive directors and ratified by a majority of member countries—was delayed in the U.S. Congress. The consensus shared by most other developed countries on the need to increase aid to developing countries seems no longer to be held by the United States.

As a financial institution, the World Bank is quite visible due to its loans to heavily indebted developing countries. In addition, as the leading institution supporting economic development in the third world, the World Bank is viewed as the main promoter of agricultural growth in developing countries, in direct competition with U.S. exports. As a result, the World Bank receives a great deal of criticism, particularly by U.S. agricultural interests.

I want to place the U.S. policy debate in a broader context. To do so, I will explain what the World Bank is, then discuss the role of agriculture in development and examine the major themes of the current international debate on agricultural, aid, trade, and development policies and, finally, discuss more precisely the current role of the World Bank in this debate.

29

WHAT IS THE WORLD BANK?

The World Bank was created at the end of World War II as part of the Bretton Woods agreements which also led to the creation of the International Monetary Fund (IMF) and the General Agreement on Tariffs and Trade (GATT). These institutions were to contribute to a new international economic order, or more precisely, to avoid the recurrence of international economic disorders such as those that occurred in the 1930s.

GATT was intended to regulate international trade policies and prevent national governments from falling back on protectionist policies. IMF was to regulate the international flows of short-term capital, thereby encouraging more stable relationships among exchange rates and discouraging aggressive devaluations.

The World Bank (formally known as the International Bank for Reconstruction and Development) was first supposed to provide long-term financial capital for the reconstruction of war-damaged economies and later for the development of poorer countries. The World Bank is international. It is made up of member governments, and has the status of an international organization. Even though its headquarters are in Washington, it is not a U.S. institution.

It secures resources on the financial market at a commercial rate. Its initial capital was provided by member governments. In addition, member governments offer their guarantees for bank borrowing on financial markets. World Bank bonds are sold in various financial centers throughout the world and are denominated in various convertible currencies. Because of its sound financial policy and member governments' guarantees, the bank has an excellent standing in world financial markets.

Now that the reconstruction of Europe has taken place, the purpose of the bank is primarily to foster development in developing countries. The distinction between developed and developing countries is, of course, variable. For the sake of clarification, developing countries today include such countries as Portugal, Romania, Poland, and Hungary.

The Bank Makes Loans to Governments in Developing Countries

In promoting economic development the bank faces certain limitations due to its specific characteristics. For example, the bank makes loans not grants. These loans must be repaid and the projects for which the loans are made must show promise of positive rates of return both in financial and economic terms.

Making long-term grants for general development purposes, however desirable and useful, is not part of the bank's mandate.

The World Bank's companion institution, the International Development Association, makes loans at low interest rates and for a long period of time. Hence there is a subsidy element in them. However, these loans are restricted to poor countries, and even these so-called "soft" loans have to be repaid no matter how concessional the terms.

The World Bank may lend only to sovereign governments or, with a government's guarantee, to institutions in a borrowing country. This constrains the bank's ability to promote development. It is particularly difficult to lend to private and voluntary organizations or farmers' groups independently of the government.

The World Bank is strict on repayment performance. It has no provision for arrears and automatically stops further disbursements to a borrowing country that is late on its payments of interest or capital on previous loans. Similarly, the World Bank has no provision for rescheduling debt.

Member Governments Determine the Bank's Policies

Decisions with regard to all operations of the bank are made by a board of executive directors comprised of representatives of member governments. These executive directors meet several times a week which means that they closely monitor the bank's activities. As a result, the institution is directly affected by the international political conditions of the world community. It suffers from the absence of a world government that would promote some form of economic rationality at the world level.

A division can often be observed between executive directors representing developed countries and those representing developing (borrowing) countries. In the past, the directors were strongly influenced by ideological differences. But the contradictions on the world scene are constantly evolving. Today a consensus is growing on the importance of market mechanisms and on limiting the role of governments in regulating economic activities. Also, there is a greater awareness of economic interdependencies at the world level.

All these specific characteristics influence what the World Bank does and the limits of its margin of maneuver. Regarding the specific power of the United States in World Bank affairs, it is important to understand that because of its share in the capital of the bank, the U.S. representative has a veto power on major decisions but not on individual loans to specific governments. All loans, in any case, must be approved by the board.

AGRICULTURE PLAYS A MAJOR ROLE IN GLOBAL DEVELOPMENT

From a global perspective, what matters is choosing an optimal strategy which will promote the fastest development of developing countries. In this context, emphasis needs to be placed on the role of agriculture in any such development strategy. Disagreement on this issue, among economists at least, seems to have been settled by now, and the importance of agriculture is well recog-

---

In most countries, agriculture should have high priority since failing to promote domestic agricultural growth results in tremendous bottlenecks in the development of other economic sectors.

---

nized. But the current financial difficulties faced by many developing countries have raised new obstacles on the course of rapid agricultural growth. Pressures from developed countries, particularly in the United States from agricultural interest groups, also have raised new constraints.

The failure of several countries that had given priority to the development of heavy, capital-intensive industry has convinced the development community that such a strategy was mistaken. In most countries, agriculture should have high priority since failing to promote domestic agricultural growth results in tremendous bottlenecks in the development of other economic sectors. These bottlenecks have been observed in countries that benefited from the oil boom in the 1970s and enjoyed high rates of economic growth, but now find it difficult to sustain that growth with lower oil prices. Algeria is a good case in point.

In addition to providing food, agriculture provides employment in economies where, typically, unemployment is raging. A significant body of empirical evidence shows that rapid agricultural growth is linked to rural economic growth. The Indian Punjab is an excellent example of this situation. But even though the role of agriculture is recognized within the development community, not all policy-makers in all countries are convinced of that role. Many pay lip service to it but, when resources are limited, they do not give priority to agriculture.

To Grow, Agriculture Needs Technology and Reliable Institutions

The conditions for agricultural growth are well-known. Agricultural growth generally requires new technologies, which increase the productivity of the limited resources. For example, the green revolution permitted large increases in the productivity of land while utilizing large quantities of labor. This fact made the green revolution well adapted to the land and labor resources available in many developing countries.

A concern for the future is that no new breakthrough analogous to the high-yielding varieties of rice and wheat of the green revolution seems to be in the pipeline. Moreover, it is not enough to have a new technology. Farmers have to be aware of it and credit for obtaining the needed inputs must be available.

A second condition for agricultural growth is the existence of or development of reliable institutions that can sustain that growth. Developing these institutions is a complex long-term process; it depends on human capital formation through training and is influenced by a country's culture and the government's political commitment.

These conditions require that resources be available to finance investments in infrastructure, education, irrigation and drainage, land consolidation and improvement, and even farm machinery and livestock. The role of the World Bank is to provide funding for these instruments.

Agricultural Development Creates Stable Markets

Serious questions have been raised about the impact of worldwide agricultural growth on developed countries. Farm interest groups, particularly in the United States, have expressed the fear that the growth of agriculture in developing countries is increasing competition with the agricultural products of developed countries. As a result, pressure has been exerted on the U.S. Agency for International Development, the World Bank, and other multilateral development institutions to interfere with that process.

It seems probable that in the short run, for some products, instances can be found of agricultural development in developing countries that, through production increases or some other improvement, hurt some agricultural interests in developed countries. However, in the long run, this development, in agriculture as well as in other sectors, is really in the general interest of developed countries.

From the standpoint of security, decreasing the gap between developed and developing countries will likely lead to greater economic, social, and political stability in the world. More directly, economic development in developing countries will create markets for developed countries, including agricultural exports.

The essential point is that rapid economic development leads to fast growth in demand for agricultural products. This demand typically increases faster than the country's agriculture can grow, particularly when people shift their diets from cereal-based to livestock-based foods. Numerous examples can be found to sup-

It seems probable that in the short run, for some products, instances can be found of agricultural developments in developing countries that, through production increases or some other improvement, hurt some agricultural interests in developed countries. However, in the long run, this development, in agriculture as well as other sectors, is really in the general interest of developed countries.

port this contention. The most dramatic prospect is southern and eastern China where several hundred million people are on the verge of rapid economic development. Whether this surge of growth will be realized, however, depends on whether the reform program recently undertaken in that country can be carried out in the long term.

International Economics Influences Agricultural Development

Agricultural development strategies such as I have described have been stymied recently by the increasing international debt of many developing countries. The magnitude of this problem can be described by the following figures: The global stock of third world debt is estimated to have increased by 3% in the past year to $1.32 trillion after having risen by 11% in the previous year to $1.28 trillion. This total level corresponds to almost 50% of the combined gross national product of developing countries. As a result, in spite of the fact that industrialized countries had steady economic growth in 1988, there has been stagnation in debtor nations. The debate on international economic policy is now centered on debt reduction strategies.

How did we arrive at this situation? Clearly the turmoils on international financial markets in the late 1970s and early 1980s had an impact. Interest rates rose sharply as well as inflation. In addition, developing countries, particularly the oil-rich countries, launched over-optimistic investment programs, borrowing liberally from world public and private markets.

Such behavior can be understood, bearing in mind the tremendous social and political pressures for economic development, resulting from the extreme poverty of large segments of the population whose aspiration levels have risen because modern media communication has transformed the world into a village. Yet many investment programs were too grandiose, and were subsequently of little value. In addition, this booming atmosphere probably led to massive, illegal capital flights from developing countries. Note that these movements contributed to financing the growing international debt of the United States, which reached $357 billion at the end of 1987.

The consequences of this situation for developing countries have been dramatic. Government expenditures have been squeezed to the point that research institutions in many countries have become paralyzed. Investments in agriculture financed by the World Bank are difficult to justify when the borrowing country is unable to meet the recurrent costs of the financed equipment or program. Thus, continued lending for long-term agricultural development has become extremely difficult.

The silver lining in this situation is a growing awareness by development authorities of the necessity to reform domestic economic policies, particularly agricultural policies, in many developing countries. In many instances these policies needed to be reformed. They implied tremendous distortions in price signals through overvalued exchange rates, taxation, and subsidies, creating a climate which hampered agricultural growth. Of those countries that have launched major policy reforms, some are beginning to bear fruit. An example is Ghana, where cocoa production had been declining under mismanaged government policies but is now improving significantly since policies have been reformed.

Another consequence of the current worldwide debt problem is that developing countries are pressuring themselves to increase exports. In order to do so, they have pushed to gain access to markets in developed countries. Chile, for example, has succeeded in exporting large amounts of fruits and vegetables to temperate-zone developed countries during the winter.

However, in most cases, developing countries face developed countries' protectionist policies, which have prevented them from exporting. Yet developing countries must be allowed to correct their balance of trade if they are to be expected to repay their debts or even to pay the interest on their debts. In this context, it is not surprising that developed countries exert conflicting pressures on the developing countries and, thus, indirectly interfere with long-term agricultural growth.

Developed Countries Influence Policy in Developing Countries

The most common pressure exerted by developed countries on developing countries is for policy reform. This pressure stems from the desire of developed countries to have their loans to developing countries repaid. The situation is made more complex by the fact that commercial banks made many loans to developing countries. Developed countries are concerned that the financial system in their own countries will collapse if too many banks were unable to meet their commitments. On the other hand, there are groups within developed countries who feel that commercial banks knowingly took risks in making these loans, cashed in on the profits from these loans, and therefore should not expect the taxpayers to bail them out.

The question of commercial bank liability aside, developed country governments generally press developing countries to reform their domestic policies to reduce excessive public spending and to get back on the path of healthy and sustainable economic growth. If there are contradictions in the behavior of developed countries, it is because numerous conflicts and specific obligations are at stake. Initiatives such as "bridge" loans have been taken unilaterally by individual governments even when such loans alleviate the pressure for adjustment. Thus, the international economic and financial game today is complex and political.

Some industries in developed countries also pressure developing countries to limit competition in specific sectors. Agreements concerning textiles, steel, and shoes are examples. The pressure exerted on agriculture is more the World Bank's concern. It is exerted primarily by the U.S. government even though, in many respects, the European agricultural policy resembles that of the United States. For example, pressures have been exerted within the United States to prevent the World Bank from lending money to Brazil to develop its soybean production. The development of palm oil production in other countries has led to similar pressures from the United States.

AGRICULTURE'S SHARE
OF WORLD BANK LENDING MAY DECLINE

In recent years the World Bank's activity has been characterized by *policy lending*. This type of lending involves quickly disbursed loans made to correct balance-of-payment deficits. Thus these loans allow developing countries to adjust their policy. Typically, policy reform will include reducing government spending, promoting exports, and reducing imports. Since imports cannot be completely halted because the social and economic costs would be too great, World Bank loans providing badly needed foreign exchange can be very useful. These loans are made on conditions of policy changes, and are referred to as *structural adjustment loans*. Somewhat similar loans, concerning only special sectors, are called *sector adjustment loans*. The share of the bank's portfolio devoted to these loans increased to 25% in the last fiscal year.

There is concern that this type of loan may contradict the objectives of the World Bank. On the one hand, investment lending (loans promoting long-term growth) is not conducive to growth if the economic environment is not appropriate. Therefore, changing the general economic environment through appropriate policy reforms appears to be the correct course of action. On the other hand, the World Bank is a development bank whose mission is to finance long-term investments. Such investments should be made on the basis of well-designed projects that can be appraised and whose implementation can be supervised. Because money is fungible, there is always the fear that quick-disbursement loans may be used to finance consumption and thus not lead to productive investments, thereby defeating the purpose of the World Bank.

It is projected that agriculture's share of total World Bank lending will continue to decline even though the total amount of funding for agriculture, expressed in nominal terms, will not decline. There are many reasons for this. Some have to do with the internal constraints of the bank, which is under great pressure to increase its lending without increasing its staff. Agricultural lending is staff-intensive.

Other reasons have to do with the status of agriculture in borrowing countries. In countries where agricultural growth has been successful, the urgency to further develop agriculture is reduced and new investment opportunities have to be invented. In Southeast Asia, for example, rice surpluses have appeared in recent years. Under this circumstance traditional investment projects such as irrigation display low economic rates of return. Rates of return are low because the international rice price is quite low, depressed in part by the policies of developed countries, particularly those of the United States. As a result, World Bank lending to agriculture in Southeast Asia countries such as Malaysia and Thailand has been reduced significantly.

In the Middle East, agricultural production is restricted by poor natural conditions. The design of suitable projects is, therefore, quite complex. In addition, expertise in both the World Bank and the Middle East is limited.

In sub-Saharan Africa, the need for agricultural investments is great. But in many cases, institutions within the countries are weak, which jeopardizes the effectiveness of lending.

In Latin America, investments are hampered by the dramatic shortage of funds available to governments for meeting the recurrent costs of investments financed through the World Bank.

Finally, with regard to trade, the consequences of developed countries' domestic policies—particularly the widespread use of export subsidies—have created havoc on world markets. Developing countries that rely on agricultural exports suffer dramatic consequences from this situation.

Other countries that need to develop their domestic agricultural production for sustainable economic growth are also hampered by low world prices. In Côte d'Ivoire, for instance, the cost of imported rice in the capital city of Abidjan is one-third the cost of irrigated rice produced in the northern part of the country. This discrepancy in price is due to the extreme difficulties and high costs of transportation that result from inadequate infrastructure. In such a case, investing in irrigation and rice production does not seem economically warranted. However, without it, the possibility of developing a sustainable growth strategy for the country is slim.

The World Bank has very little influence on international trade issues, a weakness common to all of the Bretton Woods institutions. The World Bank advocates less-distorted trade overall and freer agricultural trade in particular, since freer trade would be in the general interest of developing countries. It must be noted that this claim is not well documented. The developing countries are a heterogeneous lot and clearly the interests of the cereal-importing countries, such as Mexico, are quite different from those of the cereal-exporting countries, such as Argentina. Much work remains in exploring the potential impact of changes in trade regimes, particularly the impact of changes that would be acceptable to a majority of developed countries. The current stalemate in the GATT negotiations on agricultural trade is not favorable to developing countries.

In conclusion, the problems faced by the international community are greater than can be solved by the World Bank. The World Bank is an important actor. But, while it is directed by a board made up of representatives of national governments, it cannot substitute for a world government and cannot regulate the world economy.

MODIFYING U.S. FARM POLICY: HELPING OTHERS WHILE HELPING OURSELVES

Dale E. Hathaway
Vice President, Consultants International Group, Inc.

In 1989 and 1990 some basic and difficult decisions must be made about trade and U.S. farm policies. These decisions will come in the form of a new farm bill and in an international trade agreement—the agricultural aspects of the Uruguay Round of the multilateral trade negotiations (MTN). These decisions must be consistent because the Uruguay Round is about removing the adverse impact of domestic policies on trade—an issue that has been ignored since the founding of the General Agreement on Tariffs and Trade (GATT).

How the decisions on trade rules and domestic policy come together will have a greater effect on developing countries than the combined impact of the activities of the U.S. Agency for International Development (USAID) and the international lending institutions.

A NEW APPROACH TO FARM POLICY IS NEEDED

It is economically unrealistic and politically naive to believe that U.S. farmers will approach decisions about trade and farm policy with a major concern for the interests of farmers in the developing countries. U.S. farmers are not in the aid business; nor are the agricultural and trade committees of Congress. However, the U.S. agricultural industry can do a number of things to enhance its own well-being that will also work to the advantage of many developing countries.

In general, U.S. farm groups need to regain a sense of time perspective. In 1985, when the last farm bill was passed, the agricultural industry was wracked by deflation, a collapse in asset values, an overvalued dollar, a reduction in foreign demand, and worldwide surpluses. Now, the worst of the adjustment to these changes in the world economy and the painful deflation in farm asset prices are behind us. It is time to decide what kind of domestic farm policy and international trade policy U.S. agriculture needs for the next decade, not just next month and next year. With this in mind, I will suggest some changes in domestic policy and some directions in international trade policy which could strengthen U.S. agriculture and, incidentally, reduce or remove much of the damage being done to developing countries by the trade policies of the United States and other developed countries.

It is economically unrealistic and politically naive to believe that U.S. farmers will approach decisions about trade and farm policy with a major concern for the interests of farmers in the developing countries.

The United States Should Focus on Staying Competitive

It is clear that the United States cannot make full use of its basic agricultural capacity and that of associated businesses unless it has access to and is competitive in world markets. An attempt to withdraw to "Fortress America" in agriculture would precipitate a bloody battle in U.S. agriculture and would belie the fact that the United States claims to be a low-cost producer of a wide range of products.

In many ways, the 1985 farm bill has been successful in restoring our competitive position in world markets. However, constantly lower price supports or constant use of huge export subsidies should not be required to remain competitive.

The ability of U.S. agriculture to compete also depends on sound macroeconomic policies that keep interest rates down, prevent the dollar from being overvalued, and avoid substantial cost inflation. The macro policies which resulted in the overvalued dollar were deadly for exports as was the overkill of the 1983 payment-in-kind (PIK) program which raised U.S. and world prices at a time when demand was falling, thus giving the wrong signals to agricultural producers.

Incidentally, many developing countries also have a huge stake in U.S. macro policy because they, too, are dependent upon lower real interest rates and a stable value of the dollar.

Reduced Intervention Will Decrease Market Distortion

Between 1985 to 1988 the U.S. government intervened in local, national, and international markets more than ever before. The

42

use of PIK certificates, the export enhancement program (EEP), and other devices resulted in market distortions and made day-to-day U.S. government decisions the major factor in both the domestic and international markets. This effort to recapture lost export markets has been applauded by most farm groups and members of Congress and bitterly opposed by many U.S. competitors in the world market who have not had the benefits of virtually unlimited government funds to protect them from the market effects of these actions.

There clearly is a role for government in agriculture and I believe that most farmers and farm groups share that view. It is, however, a bit incongruent for farm groups to back a MTN proposal to eliminate all agricultural programs while backing such massive day-to-day market intervention.

While EEP is a major step toward mandated intervention, most of this market intervention is not inherent in the 1985 farm bill. As GATT rules now stand, export subsidies in agriculture are not an unfair trade practice and, therefore, they should remain in our array of trade policy alternatives as long as they are available to and used by our competitors. However, for the United States to get to the point where major importers demand export subsidies from the U.S. as a right, regardless of world supply and demand conditions, is a dangerous position for U.S. agriculture. This inevitably means that domestic and international politics rather than efficiency or good management become the major determinant of export flows. Moreover, the dominance of the United States in world markets for many products means that other suppliers must meet U.S. prices regardless of the damage it does to their farm producers and economies.

Farmers' Decisions Should Be Determined by the Market

Under recent farm programs there has been a substantial reduction in farmers' planting flexibility, which has resulted in serious production distortions. Farmers must plant their acreage of program crops and emphasize high yields to protect their acreage and yield bases. Some of the most obvious distortions arise from the administration of crop set-asides, which has resulted in sharp reductions in U.S. oilseed and oat plantings.

Many people claim that U.S. farmers are the best managers in the world and the most efficient producers of most commodities. But, U.S. farm programs are administered in ways that prohibit farmers from using their management skills. As a result, costs of production rise, the competitive position of the United States in world markets is eroded, and export subsidies must be used to maintain exports. These export subsidies are geared more to maintaining or increasing market share than to restoring world market price equilibrium. As a result, world prices decline, harming both U.S. producers and other efficient producers.

The use of land-retirement programs to withdraw excess resources from U.S. agriculture is probably the only politically acceptable way to remove excess productive capacity from U.S. agriculture. But we should remember that resources in agriculture are highly mobile and that the problem is reducing total resource use, not crop-by-crop resource use.

If there is a need for such resource restraints in the 1990s they ought to be administered in a way that decreases, not increases, inter-crop distortions. To do this, a more uniform approach to the treatment of program crops under farm programs is needed. Crops that compete in both production and consumption need to be treated in the same way. In this regard the 1985 bill was a step backward and it has resulted in serious problems within agriculture.

Farm producers should also be allowed to respond to prices. In recent years, U.S. farmers who produce program crops have been isolated from markets to an unprecedented degree. This isolation is partly due to the design of farm programs, in which target prices are immune to changes in world market prices, and partly due to program management, which has maintained local market prices well below support levels for long periods. Thus, farmers have had no real opportunity to respond to market forces; their banker told them to participate in the program, common sense told them to put their crops under loan, and their incomes depended upon the level of target prices and their ability to juggle certificates. There has been no incentive for most farmers to produce for markets, to hedge their crops, or to market carefully.

It is ironic that the United States has moved to a system that virtually removes market signals from producers' production and marketing decisions while it has criticized the European and Japanese systems of protecting their farmers from market forces and using the resources of USAID and the World Bank to encourage developing countries to move in the other direction. The United States calls itself a market economy and makes much of the inefficiencies of "non-market" economies, yet it has abandoned the use of markets in agricultural programs to an amazing degree in recent years.

Given this gross contradiction between words and action, it is not surprising that much of the world is skeptical of U.S. intentions on policy reform.

It is not necessary to "throw the baby out with the bath water."

The adverse impact of world market gyrations and unfair trading practices on farm income can be reduced without destroying the role of markets in farmers' decisions.

Farm Program Costs Should Be Reduced and Controlled

The Congress and the administration have claimed that they want to control and reduce government expenditures on agriculture. However, the 1985 farm bill, as its predecessors, was an entitlement. Each year adjustments were made in some minor details to bring its projected costs within budget targets. The actual costs, however, were dependent upon farm output, world market prices, domestic market prices, and program management.

It is doubtful President Bush will have the luxury and the Congress the flexibility to continue to provide these entitlements to U.S. agriculture when other parts of the federal budget are under extreme pressure. World financial markets will force fiscal responsibility upon the U.S. government even if the thrust of domestic politics does not. Therefore, farm program budget expenditures must be reduced and made more predictable. However, how much we spend to protect and(or) maintain farm income depends on domestic politics, world market conditions, and the macroeconomic climate.

At present, policy decisions on set-aside levels are as much a function of estimated budget exposure as world supply and demand conditions. This situation sometimes results in bad policies for U.S. farmers and it may result in hurting our competitive position, especially in a period of world market expansion. Thus, there is a need to reduce or break the link between budget decisions and farm output decisions.

It would not be especially complicated to change farm programs to increase cost predictability and control. However, since much of the recent cost variations are a direct result of macro instability, a more stable world economic environment is a key element in achieving this goal.

Farm Programs Must Meet Changing World Conditions

The droughts of 1983 and 1988 should prove to even the most skeptical observer the value of ample reserve stocks to meet unexpected changes in U.S. and foreign output and in world demand.

Our feed-grain and oilseed producers are dependent upon demand from our domestic and foreign livestock producers. In this decade U.S. corn yields have varied by as much as 50% or 40

45

bushels per acre. In this same decade the combined net imports of grain by the USSR and China have varied from a high of 60 million tons to a low of 29 million tons. To protect its own large domestic market and our export markets, the United States must be willing to ensure adequate grain and oilseed supplies to meet fluctuations in both foreign demand and domestic supply.

Nothing promotes the drive toward foreign self-sufficiency as strongly as the possibility of inadequate supplies and short-supply embargoes. While all embargoes undermine our credibility as a reliable supplier, even countries with a friendly or benign foreign policy can rightly fear a short-supply embargo. Since it is not possible to predict or control the weather in the United States or other countries, a system that allows the United States to cope with large and unpredictable changes must be maintained. For some products, markets can be regained quickly after a year of shortages and high prices, but if livestock herds are liquidated, or people in developing countries go hungry, it takes years to rebuild the markets that are lost. If other countries are driven toward self-sufficiency at all costs then the United States may never recover those markets.

Some argue that a reserve system in the United States provides an umbrella which encourages the rest of the world to expand output at the expense of U.S. producers. This argument is false on two counts. First, it is in the interest of U.S. producers to protect and expand world livestock and poultry consumption because the United States is the world's largest producer of those products and the world's largest supplier of feedstuffs. Second, the incentive for others to expand output is far less from a well-run grain reserve system than the incentive from worldwide shortages of the type experienced in the 1970s. Besides, if such a system is in the United States' best interests, why should we be bothered if, as a side effect, it also helps stabilize world markets for others?

Because of the unpredictability in agricultural production and demand—and the inherent inflexibility of mandatory supply controls—such controls are unworkable for most of U.S. agriculture. Almost by definition, they imply that the domestic market takes precedence over foreign markets. Leaving aside the issues of acceptability to farmers, the impact upon production cost and efficiency, and similar issues, these controls require either the ability to predict the unpredictable, a huge government-controlled stock program, or a retreat from world markets. None of these appears acceptable to U.S. producers or consumers.

46

U.S. AND WORLD TRADE POLICIES MUST BE COMPATIBLE

As mentioned at the outset, what happens with domestic policy will have to be compatible with what happens internationally because the world will require greater consistency from the United States in exchange for changes the United States wants from the world.

In my view, it is in the interests of both U.S. producers and those in developing countries to concentrate on removing the major distortions in world markets (as opposed to domestic markets) for major traded products. Removing distortions means two things:

- ending the use of huge direct subsidies in international markets
- taking measures to curb excess production and to guarantee market access in countries which wish to continue to price their farm products at well above world market prices

If these objectives cannot be achieved by an agreement to phase out all trade-distorting subsidies, then the articles of GATT that cover subsidies and import controls in agriculture will have to be reexamined and reformed.

Presently, several points of U.S. programs run counter to U.S. interests in greater access abroad and in fair competition in foreign markets. These programs fall under a special waiver which allows us to use import quotas without meeting the criteria under the GATT articles and EEP. The extreme reluctance of some producers to give up quota protection is rooted more in historical comfort than economic reality.

Tariffs can be used under GATT to protect domestic industries which are unable to compete. Or, as GATT rules now stand, the United States could use import quotas if it has production controls on the commodities involved and allows some guaranteed access. Thus, the choice is not to keep the present system or abandon our protected producers to unfair competition from subsidized foreign production. Our real choice is between agreeing to uniform rules for all countries or abandoning demands upon others for changes in policies that are important to the United States.

However much it is liked by some, I believe EEP could be traded off for a similar de-escalation of export subsidies by others. In any case, as suggested earlier, the EEP has its own long-run dangers for the United States which make it more useful as a bargaining chip than as a permanent policy.

It should be noted that sugar is the commodity protected by import quotas that is of major interest to developing countries.

They are not major producers of dairy products and our zero import quotas on peanuts and cotton actually protect a competitive industry which could compete without them. The willingness of the United States to consider change in some policies may determine the outcome of these negotiations. It is unrealistic to expect the rest of the world to drop their export subsidies and import barriers while the United States continues both on products of major interest to them. Target price payments on exported products also are viewed by many as a form of export subsidy, but I already have mentioned why I believe that a program should be modified to give producers more flexibility.

U.S. agriculture should drop its attack on government programs to develop agriculture and build agriculture infrastructure in developing countries. It is inconsistent for an industry that has pushed for a farm credit bailout, encouraged a $36 billion deficit in the Farmers Home Administration portfolio, expects the Corps of Engineers to insure low-cost river transport, and is heavily dependent upon federally subsidized water to sustain production of major export crops to object to public investment in agriculture elsewhere. Until the United States is willing to end these huge public investments, it is unreasonable to expect other countries to do so. Getting effective control over serious trade-distorting practices in world agriculture will be difficult. But until the United States does, attempting to limit and control basic development and farm-structure expenditures is likely to be counterproductive.

Clearly the world is not going to agree to move to a single, common system of agricultural policies. For a variety of reasons, both historical and otherwise, there will continue to be diverse structures, marketing systems, and policies. This is why U.S. farm programs must be compatible with, but not the same as, the programs of other countries.

Observers of previous GATT negotiations on agriculture could cynically expect that the present round will produce little or no results. I think that is unlikely for two reasons.

First, recent conditions in world agriculture have given agricultural policies a bad name and have almost destroyed the political and economic systems these policies were designed to protect. The world does not want to return to that situation and will make policy adjustments to avoid it.

Second, it is quite clear that we cannot have a successful GATT round in the absence of significant progress in agriculture. For many countries, agricultural trade reform is a must. This is probably true of the U.S. and the European Community and it is certainly true of the 14-nation Cairns Group, especially its developing-country members.

World political leaders will not let the GATT round fail because of agriculture. This implies that progress and choices will be made, but within the context of ongoing national policies, not in terms of abolishing them.

ALLEVIATING HUNGER
WHILE BUILDING MARKETS

John W. Mellor
Director, International Food Policy Research Institute

This paper has three objectives:

- to review the relationship between agricultural growth, overall economic growth, per capita incomes, and commercial exports
- to point to the great potentials which lie ahead in the 1990s, and to discuss why these potentials are grossly under-recognized
- to lay out an action plan to eliminate hunger and build commercial markets simultaneously over a 20-year period

EXPORT MARKETS DEPEND ON THIRD WORLD AGRICULTURAL GROWTH

With respect to commercial cereal export markets, developing countries are the only remaining growth market.

In the developed countries we see continued increases in agricultural output by about 2% a year. That is because we have institutionalized the seed varieties, chemicals, and production methods that increase agricultural productivity. Thus, inevitably, supply moves ahead of demand and either exportable surpluses are generated, storage stocks are increased, or resources have to be withdrawn from agriculture at an uncomfortably rapid pace.

These processes now are beginning to occur in the Soviet Union. So far, their demand for cereals has been growing rapidly, particularly due to a rapid growth in livestock consumption that has moved ahead of the moderate pace of agricultural production growth—a pace which has been faster than that of western Europe. Eventually, demand growth will slow. At that point, the Soviet Union will move towards self-sufficiency and the United States will lose this export market.

In developed countries like the United States, incomes have been raised to the point at which people do not wish to consume significantly more food even when their incomes rise. In the developing countries of the world, incomes are so low that as incomes grow food demand increases rapidly and continues to do so for many decades. It is possible to raise incomes and hence food consumption of people in developing countries so rapidly that, when combined with rapid population growth, food demand will outstrip even the most rapid rates of food production growth that are possible. That will create substantial commercial markets if the capacity to pay for those food imports is created.

There are four key points to keep in mind with respect to income growth and the eventual creation of commercial markets:

- The mass of the people in developing countries live in rural areas.
- If agricultural growth can be accelerated in the rural areas where all these people are located, it will increase both employment and incomes, as well as output from the rural sector.
- Agricultural growth is the best way to incorporate this mass of rural people into the development process. The cost of moving rural people into nonagricultural jobs in the major metropolitan centers is too high. Countries that have tried have ended up with unequal income distributions and relatively slow growth.
- The United States will not be able to capture all of these third world export markets. Developing countries will generate exportable surpluses in some agriculture commodities, while at the same time importing others. The imports will be much greater than the exports. If the United States concentrates on eliminating the export competition, the growth processes which bring about the import potentials may be lost.

There are exceptions to the generalization that agricultural growth must be the basis on which the overall growth occurs. The two key exceptions are Hong Kong and Singapore. They are both city-states which lack a major agricultural sector. That is not characteristic of developing countries generally. The third exception is South Korea, which first developed its industrial sector and then that pulled the agricultural sector along. However, South Korea was peculiar in two respects. Most important was that the extremely large quantities of capital needed to move the industrial sector without support from agriculture were provided by massive capital imports. Those capital imports were way beyond what could be sustained in most developing countries. Second, South Korea had preferred access to the largest and most rapidly growing industrial market in the world—the United States.

ECONOMIC GROWTH POTENTIAL
IS HIGH IN THE 1990s

The 1960s and 1970s constituted a period of rapid economic growth in developing countries. The growth rates slowed to a crawl and almost stopped towards the middle of the 1980s. Even in the latter part of the 1980s only a few Asian countries had returned to the rapid growth of the 1960s and 1970s. Two points must be kept in mind in assessing the potential markets for the 1990s:

• It is not surprising that economic growth slowed in the 1980s. The oil shocks, the rapid inflation that was associated with the United States' participation in the Vietnam War, and a number of related factors resulted in major structural distortions throughout the global economy in the 1980s. In order to bring those distortions under control and create a favorable basis for eventual return to growth, the growth processes themselves slowed to a halt in the 1980s. A rapid cessation of monetary growth in the United States, the debt crisis and attempts to get that under control, and other forces slowed the growth process.

• The basic engine of growth is not foreign trade, but the development of human resources. A productive labor force combined with effective institutions allows technological change and productivity growth to proceed. The processes of human resource formation were proceeding rapidly through the 1980s throughout the developing world, even in Africa where the actual growth rate was so disastrously low. A much larger stock of human resources provides the basis for faster growth in the 1990s than was possible in the 1960s and 1970s.

Elimination of the distortions of the 1980s—and the growth in the stock of human resources and the institutional structures to utilize it—offer a favorable prospect for the 1990s.

FOOD AID PLUS ECONOMIC GROWTH
CAN ALLEVIATE HUNGER

One way to alleviate hunger is to use large quantities of food in the short run, and also stimulate economic growth which would allow for a rapid growth of commercial markets in the long run.

Who Are the Poor and Hungry?

The first questions that must be raised when talking about alleviating hunger through economic development and creating commercial markets are who are the poor and hungry, where are they located, and how many of them are there.

By the usual definition of absolute poverty at the level of severe caloric deprivation, there are about 700 million people below that miserably low poverty line. A somewhat more reasonable poverty line indicates there are about one billion people who are hungry and poor.

These people are located largely in rural areas. Ninety percent of the hungry poor in Africa are in rural areas as are 80% in Asia. Even in Latin America, which is very urbanized, 60% of the hungry poor are in rural areas.

Most striking about the hungry poor is that a substantial proportion of them—about 250 million—are located in rural areas that have a high potential for agricultural growth. These areas have been productive enough to support a large but very poor population. Rapid population growth has occurred in these areas precisely because they are productive. Because they are productive, they offer potential for the application of new high-yielding varieties that can raise incomes and food supplies, and lift the hungry poor out of their extreme poverty.

Innovations and Infrastructure Are Catalysts for Growth

What needs to be done to avail of these opportunities? There are two key elements:

- technological innovations that allow an increase in productivity, particularly in yields per acre of the scarce, valuable, highly productive land
- infrastructure that allows those commercially viable technological innovations to move out over the whole rural area

Studies of infrastructure show that rural areas that do not have access to all-weather roads and the institutional structures that go along with them are left out of the development process.

The cost of providing accessible roads to all rural people in developing countries is about $300 billion. The distribution lines for rural electrification and rural telephones would add some 10% to that cost, for a total of less than $350 billion.

Two caveats need to be kept in mind if this figure seems overwhelming:

- Somewhere between 15% and 40% of the cost of building that infrastructure is represented by the food consumed by the people building it; labor-intensive processes are the most appropriate ones for producing this infrastructure. Large food surpluses could be used for this purpose, providing the goods upon which

54

the incomes of laborers building that infrastructure could be spent.
• If infrastructure along with ancillary improvements were provided over a 20-year period, it would amount to about $15 billion per year.

The program to eliminate hunger described above could be described as a 20-20-20 program. Twenty billion dollars a year to

---

Thus there is great opportunity for U.S. agriculture to do well while doing good. To do so in this complex world requires understanding complex processes and effective policies that will work to alleviate hunger and create markets.

---

pay for infrastructure, 20 million tons of food aid a year to provide the food for that labor force, and a 20-year period. The 20-year period should be seen as combining 5 years for building up the capacity for the program, 10 years of steady activity, and 5 years of gradual decline in program activity.

The cost of such an effort could be shared with developing countries. Perhaps they could pick up half of it. The costs, of course, are immense. The $20 billion is equal to a little more than half of the total of current annual foreign assistance from developed to developing countries. The food aid involved would be three times the present food aid level. Thus seriousness of purpose and resolve would be required in order to build the rural institutional structures for such a massive effort.

Now is the time for such an effort. It would not have been possible 20 years ago because many other factors besides building this basic infrastructure were necessary, but not available. For example, all the vital institutions of technological change hardly existed 20 years ago. Now, most of those are being provided at somewhere near an appropriate scale. Again, now is the time to put on the massive push for the infrastructure.

THE UNITED STATES CAN DO WELL WHILE DOING GOOD

If the United States is serious about alleviating hunger through economic development and growth and creating commercial markets in the long run, three critical needs have to be met:

- Foreign assistance must be substantially increased and focused on the countries where the bulk of the poorest people are located.
- Foreign assistance must have a major food component.
- Developing countries must recognize the need for adequate food supplies for their people and plan to give greater emphasis to agriculture, rural development, and employment.

The risk that programs may be discontinued must be reduced by effective food security programs. These programs include putting food aid on a more stable basis and reinvigorating the now more or less moribund International Monetary Fund cereal facility which provides loans to developing countries to meet their critical food imports in times of scarcity.

It must be recognized that a substantial amount of the commercial demand for cereals imports will come on the livestock feed side and not the human food side. At the same time that the potential market is tapped for vast quantities of livestock feed, the livestock industry in developing countries can provide a tremendous increase in employment and hence demand for food for direct consumption. If it is to prosper, the livestock industry needs substantial technical assistance in production, storage, transportation, and other aspects of marketing. Technical assistance to the livestock industry should form a major part of a foreign assistance program.

Thus there is great opportunity for U.S. agriculture to do well while doing good. To do so in this complex world requires understanding complex processes and effective policies that will work to alleviate hunger and create markets.

APPENDIX 1

WORKSHOP PARTICIPANTS
U.S. AID, TRADE, AND FARM POLICIES:
WORKING TOGETHER IN THE 1990s

Steve Abrams
LEG/CLS
Room 2895NS
USAID
Washington, DC 20523

Duane Acker
Assistant to the Administrator
U.S. Agency for International
   Development
A/AID, Room 5883 State NS
320 21st Street, N.W.
Washington, DC 20523-0063

Kenneth L. Bader
President and CEO
American Soybean Association
777 Craig Road
P.O. Box 27300
St. Louis, MO 63141

Dick Blue
Consultant
2170 Rayburn House Office Building
Washington, DC 20515

N.C. Brady
Senior Assistant Administrator
Bureau for Science and Technology
State Department Building
Room 4942
Washington, DC 20523

Janet Breslin
Majority Deputy Staff Director
Committee on Agriculture, Nutrition,
   and Forestry
Dirksen Senate Office Building
Washington, DC 20510

Anita Brown
Professional Staff Member
House Committee on Agriculture
1301 Longworth House Office Building
Washington, DC 20515

Eugene Chiavarola
Deputy Assistant Administrator
Bureau for Science and Technology
USAID
Washington, DC 20523-0057

Philip Christenson
Senate Foreign Relations Committee
452 Dirksen Senate Office Building
Washington, DC 20510

Richard Cobb
Deputy Director Technical Resources
   Office, ANE/TR
USAID
22nd and C Streets, N.W.
Washington, DC 20523

Lynn M. Daft
Abel, Daft, and Earley
1410 King Street
Alexandria, VA 22314

John Datt
American Farm Bureau Federation
600 Maryland Avenue, S.W.
Suite 800
Washington, DC 20024

William M. Dietel
1611 North Kent Street
Suite 600
Arlington, VA 22209

Harold Dodd
President
Illinois Farmers Union
40 Adloff Lane, Suite 1
Springfield, IL 62703

Mary Kilgour
Deputy Assistant Administrator
USAID FVA/FFP
402 SA-8
Washington, DC 20523

Marvin Duncan
Acting Chairman
Farm Credit Administration
1501 Farm Credit Drive
McLean, VA 22102-5090

Cooper Evans
314 Main Street
P.O. Box 278
Cedar Falls, IA 50613

Robert M. Frederick
Legislative Director
National Grange
1616 H Street, N.W.
Washington, DC 20006

Ron Gollehon
President
Agricultural Cooperative Development
    International
50 F Street, N.W., Suite 900
Washington, DC 20001

Margaret Goodman
Staff Consultant
House Committee on Foreign Affairs
2170 Rayburn House Office Building
Washington, DC 20515

Randy Green
WETEC
National Association of Wheat Growers
415 Second Street, N.E.
Suite 300
Washington, DC 20002

Clifford M. Hardin
10 Roan Avenue
St. Louis, MO 63124

Dale Hathaway
Vice President
Consultants International Group, Inc.
1616 H Street, N.W.
Washington, DC 20006

Robert Havener
President
Winrock International
Rt. 3, Petit Jean Mountain
Morrilton, AR 72110

Raymond Hopkins
Chair, Political Science Department
Swarthmore College
Swarthmore, PA 19081

George M. Ingram
Senior Staff Consultant
Committee on Foreign Affairs
Rayburn House Office Building
Washington, DC 20515

Jack Jenkins
11816 Great Owl Circle
Reston, VA 22094

Stanley R. Johnson
Professor of Economics
Center for Agricultural and Rural
    Development
Iowa State University
578 Heady Hall
Ames, IA 50011

Alan Kemper
First Vice President
National Corn Growers Association
5710 E 700 South
Lafayette, IN 47905

Dean R. Kleckner
President
American Farm Bureau Federation
225 Touhy Avenue
Park Ridge, IL 60068

Debbie Krumme
Technical Writer
Winrock International
Rt. 3, Petit Jean Mountain
Morrilton, AR 72110

John Lee
ERS, USDA
Room 1226
1301 New York Avenue, N.W., Room 1226
Washington, DC 20005-4788

Kristi Livingston
Evans and Associates
Washington, DC

John Maguire
Vice President Washington Operations
National Cotton Council of America
1110 Vermont Avenue
Suite 410
Washington, DC 20005

Jerre Manarolla
FVA/PPM SA-8 Room 220
USAID
Washington, DC 20523

John Mellor
Director
IFPRI
1776 Massachusetts Avenue, N.W.
Washington, DC 20036

Jim Miller
Past President
National Association of Wheat Growers
P.O. Box 233
Garfield, WA 99130

58

Jon O'Rourke
Chief, Policy Analysis Division
Office of Program Policy & Management
Bureau for Food for Peace and Voluntary
    Assistance
USAID, Room 211, SA-8
Washington, DC 20523

Cliff Ouse
National Rural Electric Cooperative
    Association
1800 Massachusetts Avenue, N.W.
Washington, DC 20036

Robert L. Paarlberg
Associate Professor
Wellesley College
Department of Political Science
Wellesley, MA 02181

Michel Petit
Director
Agricultural and Rural Development
The World Bank
18th and Pennsylvania
Washington, DC 20433

Jim Phippard
Senate Committee on Agriculture,
    Nutrition, and Forestry
328-A Russell Senate Office Building
Washington, DC 20510-6000

Gerald E. Pitchford
Staff Consultant
Committee on Foreign Affairs
2170 Rayburn House Office Building
Washington, DC 20515

Don Reeves
Agricultural Policy Analyst
Bread for the World
802 Rhode Island Avenue, N.E.
Washington, DC 20018

Susan Sechler
Ford Foundation
1333 New Hampshire Avenue, N.W.
Suite 1070
Washington, DC 20036

Kennard O. Stephens
Director International Trade Servicing
U.S. Feed Grains Council
1400 K Street, N.W., Suite 1200
Washington, DC 20005

Wayne E. Swegle
Director of Public Affairs and
    Communication
Winrock International
Rt. 3, Petit Jean Mountain
Morrilton, AR 72110

Charles Sykes
Director of Washington Liaison Office
CARE
2025 I Street, N.W.
Suite 1001
Washington, DC 20006

Doyle Talkington
National Pork Producers Council
1015 Fifteenth Street, N.W.
Suite 402
Washington, DC 20005

Milton Thomas
President
Arkansas Farmers Union
1520 West 12th Street
Little Rock, AR 72200

Dr. Robert L. Thompson
Dean of Agriculture
AGAD
Purdue University
West Lafayette, IN 47907

Steve Wentworth
President
National Corn Growers Association
RR 1
Oreana, IL 62554

Steve Wingert
Deputy Director, Technical Service
Bureau of Latin America and the
    Caribbean/DR
USAID
Washington, DC 20523

Alan Woods
Administrator
USAID
320 21st Street, N.W.
Washington, DC 20523

APPENDIX 2

SUGGESTED READING ON AID, TRADE, AND FARM POLICIES

Angel, Bruna, Tom Harrington, W.H. Meyers, and S.R. Johnson. 1989. Economic Growth and Agricultural Trade of Less-Developed Countries: Summary Report. Staff Report 89-SR37. Center for Agricultural and Rural Development, Iowa State University, Ames, IA, USA.

Clubb, Deborah and Polly C. Ligon (eds.). 1989. Food, Hunger, and Agricultural Issues. Development Education Series. Winrock International Institute for Agricultural Development. Morrilton, AR, USA.

E.A. Jaenke & Associates. 1987. Third World: Customers or Competitors? A Source Book on Agricultural Development and Trade. Washington, DC, USA.

Lee, J.E., Jr., and M. Shane. 1985. United States Agricultural Interests and Growth in the Developing Economies: The Critical Linkage. Economic Research Service, U.S. Department of Agriculture, Washington, DC, USA.

Mellor, John W. 1988. Agricultural Development in the Third World: The Food, Development, Foreign Assistance, Trade Nexus. Reprint no. 124. International Food Policy Research Institute, Washington, DC, USA.

National Planning Association, Food and Agriculture Committee. 1987. U.S. Agriculture and Third World Economic Development: Critical Interdependency. NPA report no.6, FAC report no. 223. Washington, DC, USA.

Paarlberg, R.L. 1987. U.S. Agriculture and the Developing World: Partners or Competitors? In: R. Purcell and E. Morrison (eds.). U.S. Agriculture and Third World Development: The Critical Linkage. Lynne Rienner Publishers, Inc., Boulder, CO, USA. pp. 221-241.

Smuckler, Ralph H. and Robert J. Berg with David F. Gordon. 1988. New Challenges, New Opportunities: U.S. Cooperation for International Growth and Development in the 1990s. Center for Advanced Study of International Development, Michigan State University, East Lansing, MI, USA.

Vocke, Gary. March 1987. Economic Growth, Agricultural Trade, and Development Assistance. USDA-ERS Agriculture Information Bulletin no. 509. U.S. Government Printing Office, Washington, DC, USA.

Woods, Alan. 1989. Development in the National Interest: U.S. Economic Assistance into the 21st Century. United States Agency for International Development, Washington, DC, USA.

APPENDIX 3

FOOD AND AGRICULTURE GOALS, DIRECTIONS, AND OPERATIONS FOR THE 1990s

A statement by the
U.S. Agency for International Development
March 30, 1989

This statement responds to charges by Administrator Alan Woods to outline a "single, fully coordinated set of policies and programmatic directions" in food and agriculture, steps for developing a strong working relationship with the U.S. agribusiness community and with groups that are concerned with international food issues, and, once programmatic directions were outlined, implementation steps U.S. Agency for International Development (USAID) should take, especially in food aid/agricultural program linkages and in science and technology/field program linkages.

USAID handles food and agriculture development programs in about 70 third world countries, which are usually referred to as less-developed countries (LDCs). USAID's central mission is to carry out legislative provisions for LDC development; to help LDCs achieve broad-based, sustainable economic growth and self reliance; to raise household income; and to improve the human condition—the nutrition, health, education, and physical and mental productivity of men, women, and children. USAID thereby contributes to world stability and advances U.S. foreign policy. U.S. citizens' concerns for human welfare, for poverty alleviation, for free world trade, and for the world's environment and natural resources are foundations for this central mission.

USAID's food and agriculture program is critical to fulfilling that mission. And there is urgency—rapidly increasing population pressure on fragile natural resources, worldwide, but especially in Africa—during a time when U.S. budget resources are limited.

The statement is based on USAID's experience in helping countries develop, U.S. budget realities, and the principle that U.S. investments in LDCs should be based on mutual interests.

Both direct and indirect input has been provided by USAID's mission and Washington staff (especially the deputy assistant administrators [DAAs] and key bureau staff they chose), respected economists, development professionals inside and outside USAID, LDC professionals and leaders, and U.S. industry and interest group leaders.

This statement is consistent with existing USAID policy and strategy documents. For food and agriculture programs, it outlines USAID's goals, the preference for food self-reliance over self-sufficiency, where investment pays off, the directions programs should move, and what USAID needs to do to move in the needed direction and to have most positive development impact.

LDCs AND THE UNITED STATES: MUTUAL INTERESTS

Self-sufficiency in food production for LDCs is not in the maximum economic interest of most LDCs. Nor is it in the interest of the United States.

Food self-reliance for LDCs—food security achieved from production and(or) imports, the ratio depending on comparative advantage—is in the economic interest of both LDCs and the United States.

Maintenance and enhancement of the world's environment and the natural resource base are in the interest of both LDCs and the United States.

Where significant economic growth has occurred in LDCs, agricultural development has generally been the key first step. In many countries, food aid has contributed to the process, providing calories and nutrients for human survival and productivity until and while agricultural development occurs.

Where significant economic growth has occurred in LDCs, demand for more and higher-quality food has increased sharply.

In most LDCs, 50% to 80% of the workers are farmers. When their productivity goes up, the total country economy benefits. When caloric and critical nutrient intake go up, both physical and mental well-being and productivity are enhanced.

Farmers are generally the largest sector of employment; increased productivity here has most impact on the total country economy.

When the farm family produces extra food, it is sold or bartered to obtain both inputs and consumer goods, and thereby generates employment. That food enhances nutrition in villages and urban areas; human productivity there is increased. Both the nutritional and economic impacts spread, to the towns and cities, and stimulate the growth and productivity of agribusiness, processing, manufacturing, and services.

Such agriculturally led development commonly results in 3% to 7% annual growth in gross national product (GNP) and in consumer demand in advancing LDCs. Rarely though, does LDC food production grow more than 2.5% per year. Continued population and family income growth in such advancing LDCs usually combine to increase demand for more food than their agricultural systems can provide. That is why LDCs are the growth market for U.S. agriculture. And why more growth potential lies ahead.

The United States enjoys a strong reputation in food and agriculture. Productive soil, temperate climate, a good research and education system, infrastructure, and strong private enterprise have made the U.S. agriculture system, as a whole, the envy of the world. USAID and its predecessors have effectively used some of this system's output, especially its capable men and women, universities, and food surpluses to help the LDCs.

In food and agriculture development efforts, USAID has had positive impact. The food calories and nutrients, plus the genetic materials, technology, training, credit systems, design of infrastructure, and policy support, have helped many LDCs achieve economic growth. Real family incomes have gone up.

In short, in food and agriculture as a whole, the United States enjoys a comparative advantage. It has a reservoir of talent and experience that LDCs need.

This mutuality of interest—the nutritional needs and food demand growth potential of the LDCs matched with the market growth needs and production capacity of U.S. agriculture—dictate that U.S. efforts to achieve economic growth in LDCs place a high priority on food and agriculture programs and resultant U.S. food and agriculture exports.

There is a second form of mutual interest in the agriculture arena— the two-way movement of genetic material and technology. In the early years of USAID's agricultural development, emphasis was on movement and adaptation of U.S. technology and genetic materials to the LDCs.

In more recent years, with recognition of the narrow genetic base of many U.S. crops and the diversity of germplasm in LDCs, many of them the original home of U.S.-grown crops, increased attention has focused on preserving that diverse material and its availability to U.S. agriculture.

Also, agricultural research capacity around the world is growing. Currently, that are 15 or more international agricultural research centers, national agricultural research systems in both the developed and advancing developing countries, and a growing number of intercountry commodity or topic research networks. This suggests that the United States is no longer the uncontested leader or self-sufficient in agricultural technology.

Intensity of world competition in agriculture and dependence of U.S. agriculture on exports make it exceedingly important that U.S. agriculture have access to diverse genetic material and technology, wherever it may exist or be developed.

U.S. agriculture must have worldwide technology and genetic-material linkages to that technology; USAID's programs can help foster those linkages.

There is mutual U.S. and LDC interest in the environment and natural resources. Rapidly expanding populations in the LDCs put intense pressure on fragile natural resources. Intensive cropping and grazing may leave soil denuded much of the year, allowing soil erosion and resultant siltation of streams and reservoirs.

Demand for fuelwood has dissipated timber resources.

All the world's residents benefit from maintenance of the natural resources, the diversity of the genetic base, and a clean and healthful environment.

The United States also enjoys a comparative advantage in technology and management capability for the natural resources. Its research and educational institutions, its educated and experienced men and women, and its management systems are admired worldwide.

These common interests—the vast needs of LDCs and the necessity of sustainable world environment—match well the U.S. environmental interests and capacities.

Goals

During the past 2 years, a focus statement for USAID's Agriculture Rural Development and Nutrition program was devised and has helped guide program development. This brief statement, which expresses the goals of the USAID's Food and Agriculture Program, is

To increase the income of the poor majority,
And expand the availability and consumption of food,
While maintaining and enhancing the natural resource base.

Every program or project in the food and agriculture area is expected to have positive, direct, or indirect impact for one or more (usually two or three) of the goals; negative impact for none.

These goals are central to assessing program success. With some projects and programs, impacts are short-term, direct, and traceable. Where demonstrable impact requires a long time (this is common in development effort), progress indicators that are credibly related to the goals should be assessed.

Increasing income of the poor majority. Because LDC economic growth is essential in order to finance sustained human progress, and because income is the major determinant of food consumption among low-income people, increased real family income is USAID's primary goal.

The increased family income sought (real income to the households) includes both cash and non-cash, farm and non-farm, and rural and urban incomes. Though there is variance among LDCs in family income levels, all need higher family incomes to achieve the GNP that will provide the level and quality of goods and services people seek. At all income levels, income is the major determinant of human choices.

Emphasis is placed on increasing income of the poor majority because it is at the lower family income levels that increasing income has the most beneficial impact on human welfare and food consumption. Where per capita income is $50 to $400, 50 to 60 cents of each dollar increase in income is usually spent for food. Increased income enhances food security for both the family and the country.

Food aid, whether provided in a school feeding program or maternal/child clinic to enhance nutrition, or used as payment for work, is also an income source. It frees money that can be used for seed, fertilizer, school books, or other items. It also builds human capital, through better health and education, contributing to later income growth.

Agriculture creates real income. It converts sunlight, human labor, and the elements to consumable or salable commodities. Strengthening an agriculture system increases real income.

Income and the resultant demand generate employment. Employment generates income. Family income is both a component and a consequence of country economic growth.

Export income is also important to a country. Commodities or products for which a country enjoys competitive advantage can be exported. Exports generate foreign exchange, which finances imports that people want and need, contributing to the self-reliance that every country seeks.

Expand food availability and consumption. When caloric intake goes from 1200 per day toward 1500 or 2000 and the diet provides adequate levels of quality protein, iron, vitamin A and other nutrients, the health, physical productivity, and mental productivity of men, women, and children increase.

Food aid to low-income populations, government policies that stimulate and reward food production, agricultural research and education, efforts to preserve soil and water resources, and investments in roads to move both food and production inputs, all help.

Especially as incomes in developing countries increase, nutritional quality, food processing, and other consumption-enhancing technologies and industries warrant attention.

Whereas vitamin A administration in certain geographic areas provides a temporary cure for night blindness, prevention of night blindness and the more serious consequences of prolonged vitamin A deficiency will occur only when education, tradition, and vegetable supplies insure diets that are adequate in vitamin A.

Absolute food self-sufficiency for LDCs is not a U.S. objective. Most countries' comparative advantages do not perfectly parallel their food demands. A country's economic status and progress are usually better served by exporting items for which it has a comparative advantage and importing those for which it does not. That helps a country achieve self-reliance in food and other goods.

Food self-sufficiency may be an objective expressed by an LDC country leader. In countries with a history of food shortage, that objective attracts much political support. But U.S. objectives emphasize food self-reliance—assuring food security by utilizing both in-country production and international trade.

These first two goals point to opportunity for long-term increases in exports of U.S. agricultural commodities.

Maintain and enhance the natural resource base. That part of the environment that is the foundation for sustainable agriculture—the soil, water, plant and animal species, essential minerals, and other resources—are under intense population pressure in most LDCs. Food aid can diminish that pressure, at least until technology, training, credit, genetic materials, or other advances allow increased production and good policies to stimulate production and trade. Those policies and technologies can and must help preserve topsoil, soil nutrients and structure, rangeland, coastal water and marine resources, and forest land; and keep the water, streams, estuaries and lakes free from adulterants.

Effects on the climate and on the diversity of genetic materials must be positive or neutral, not negative, in both the short-run and the long-run.

The resource base can sometimes be enhanced. Imported phosphorus can be added to the soil; organic matter can be increased by alley cropping or minimum tillage and crop rotation. Fragile soils can be released from food grain production and returned to grass or trees in those geographic areas where technology allows food needs to be met through more intensive production without degradation on the better soils.

Directions

Countries are advancing. Many LDCs have made development progress and will make more.

Continued effort by USAID toward increased production of basic food crops is still critical in many countries, but in others much progress has been made in technology implementation, production systems, and research capability.

Technologies that will contribute most to increasing income and jobs when daily caloric intake is 2500 and per capita income is $800 (technologies for animal protein production, food processing, packaging, and input agribusiness) will likely be different from those needed most when caloric intake was 1200 and income was $65 (technologies for rice, root crops, or wheat production).

Institutions whose strengthening will most impact income or other goals may be different as countries advance—perhaps agribusiness organizations, market news, and commercial banks, which parallel earlier efforts to strengthen farmer cooperatives or intermediate credit institutions for small farmers. Perhaps a strengthened vegetable or poultry research unit is needed to complement earlier food and feed grain research.

In some advanced LDCs, revised export/import policies may now have the most effect on increasing GNP, after farm price policy changes have stimulated production.

In some developing countries (South Korea, Indonesia, Thailand, and Pakistan, for example), there has been real growth in family incomes, per capita food consumption has increased, diets are more diversified, and people now seek and can afford higher quality, more nutritious, and increased quantities of processed foods. Food processing industries mean more employment. Consistent quality of processed food attracts foreign sales. There are more opportunities for export and trade, which also can mean more jobs.

To continually have the most impact toward the goals, USAID's food and agriculture programs must move in the direction of LDC country advancement. Programs should move in these directions:

• sustainable agriculture in all settings
• animal agriculture, aquaculture, and horticulture as consumer incomes and demand rise
• food processing, packaging, and distribution as urbanization proceeds
• consumption and nutrition enhancement as the food supply becomes less of a limiting factor
• agricultural businesses as specialization increases in the agricultural sector
• private sector research and technology initiatives as incentives and capacity appear
• international trade as comparative advantages become evident

The food and agriculture programs must move as the greater opportunity for impact moves in each country. To contribute most toward the goals of income, availability and consumption of food, and status of the natural resource base, talent needs within USAID will shift.

The directions outlined above do not automatically call for stopping or diminishing other USAID efforts in a region, subregion, or country. And, unfortunately, some countries are not advancing in income and food availability.

But as development proceeds in an advancing LDC, USAID must direct its food and agriculture efforts to help that LDC take the next step (for example, increased production of animal protein or development of agribusinesses and food processing), while that country assumes major responsibility for solidifying achievements in such areas as basic food crop production.

Timing is critical. The time to shift mission programs in each country or to close out major programs and shift resources to other countries, depends on many factors. The responsibility to assess these factors rests on both USAID's mission staff and Washington staff (AID/W) working closely with host-country leaders.

Operational Areas for Major USAID Investment

USAID's experience, LDC needs, and U.S. interests point toward four operational areas where there has been and where there will be the most positive impact toward the three goals of income, food availability and consumption, and status of the national resource base. The four areas are

• Country policies that stimulate broad-based economic growth, food consumption, and maintenance of natural resources
• Institutions that lead, educate, and support
• Technology, both development and transfer to users
• The private sector, where creativity and motivation yield the most economic progress

Investments in these areas, as countries advance, must be increasingly in the directions outlined in the previous section.

Note that in discussions below for each of the investment areas, investments in people are emphasized. It is largely through advancing human capacity—nutrition, health, knowledge—that countries advance. The United States has a strong comparative advantage in education and training.

Country policies that stimulate growth. The correct price, taxation, or investment policies stimulate production, private investment, trade, food consumption, and preservation and prudent use of timber and other natural resources.

USAID emphasizes graduate and continuing education in policy concepts and principles, studies that identify needed policy change, and dialogue and negotiation with food aid as an incentive for policy change (coordinated with policy efforts of the World Bank and other lenders).

Policy change is not easy, and there are risks, but the right policies have positive ripple impact on the total development process.

Institutions. This includes government units for data gathering, policy making, budgeting, market reporting, building and maintaining roads; farm-level and market-level organizations and institutions, indigenous private and voluntary organizations (PVOs), and industry and business organizations; and education and research institutions that a country can sustain. It includes graduate and continuing education to enhance the knowledge, skills, and productivity of people who staff these institutions. The benefits are long term, perpetuating, and sustainable.

Technology development and transfer. The research and education institutions previously mentioned are central, but the need also includes identifying and accessing technology that is available globally. It includes networking with international centers and other countries' research and education institutions, developing the tradition of investing in technology, rewarding scientists, and developing technology transfer systems that fit the country and its needs.

The private sector. Beyond government policies that stimulate growth, there is opportunity to strengthen private sector credit, contracting, marketing, management, and standards of performance in most LDCs.

In many LDCs, government is considered the patron and provider; parastatals that respond less to market signals abound. Yet, creativity and motivation reside in people, and the private sector most effectively lets people contribute most to economic growth.

Joint and cooperative efforts with the U.S. Trade and Development Program, the Overseas Private Investment Corporation (OPIC), and both LDC and U.S. private-sector entities must be pursued.

RESOURCES AND THEIR ALLOCATION

Whereas the United States invested about 2.5% of its GNP during the Marshall Plan years to help economic reconstruction and growth of Western Europe, only about 0.25% of U.S. GNP is invested today to help achieve economic growth of LDCs. Reconstruction of Western Europe was then deemed vital to the economic future of the United States. Today, broad-based economic growth of LDCs is vital to the future of the United States.

Increased U.S. investments for LDC development, especially in the food and agriculture sector, are clearly warranted to best serve both U.S. and LDC interests.

It is ironic that U.S. investments that can help develop trading partners in the world's most populous regions with the most consumption growth potential have been declining at a time when the United States is suffering prolonged and severe negative trade balance, and its traditional agricultural export markets are mature, and agricultural production and export capacity remain awesome.

There will always be a limit, however, to appropriated dollars, local currency, and food aid as spendable development resources. Such limits dictate focusing USAID's food and agriculture effort as outlined on previous pages.

USAID will leave to multilateral lending agencies, because of their larger resources, the major role in capital investments in infrastructure, such as railroads, major road systems, major processing and manufacturing facilities, and major irrigation systems. USAID will contribute to policy, management, and related issues where appropriate. It will defer to the private sector in those enterprises where potential reward adequately stimulates investment, such as intensive poultry and swine enterprises in some countries, but it will provide support to these sectors through policy, technology, institutions, and other means. It will depend on other bilateral and multilateral donors to pursue those endeavors for which they may have comparative advantage and available resources.

USAID will assist infrastructure development in specific ways, such as supporting government investment policies, education and training, and food-for-work programs.

Food aid deserves special recognition as a resource. Though there is often high cost to its use—ocean transport and moving it in-country to target populations, inventory control, and auditing its use—some development experts point to instances where food has especially significant development impact. A food-for-work project may improve family nutrition, serve as income transfer (money not spent for food can be used for seeds or school books) and build roads or plant trees.

In addition to insuring that family nutrition goes up, it may provide a family labor market (building the road or planting the trees) that would not otherwise exist. It is better to achieve a road that will serve community trade and culture than to give the food and have no road.

Food aid can be a disincentive to production. But its use has generally been and should be directed to programs and circumstances where it is not. Research by the International Food Policy Research Institute suggests many circumstances, in fact, where food aid can be sharply increased without disincentive effect.

Food aid can also be used as a crutch by a receiving government that has not provided adequate policy or financial investment in agriculture.

Dependability and consistency in resources, in both dollars and food aid, are also important. Development is a fragile process; continuity is critical. Each development step builds on the previous step. Interruption—of either dollars or food aid—is costly, to both the process and to the LDC leaders and their people. At all levels, confidence that the next step can be taken adds motivation to taking the first step, whether it is building an experiment station, a road, or a government policy. Multi-year food aid agreements (subject, of course, to appropriations and food availability) can enhance that confidence, at least paralleling the confidence that exists in the case of Development Assistance (DA) or Economic Support Funds (ESF).

Resources also include contractors and grantees—universities, PVOs, cooperatives, corporations, associations, and others—which help USAID get its job done.

Rapid urbanization in LDCs prompts the question if USAID's resources now assigned to the agricultural sector (including rural development, nutrition, and natural resources) should not be shifted to the needs of the masses of people in large urban centers, such as health, water, sewers, streets, and education. Large needs certainly exist, but moving resources from the agricultural sector is strongly advised against.

The overriding purpose is development. Investments in urban centers tend to be largely consumptive, with more humanitarian and less development impact. Investments in the agricultural sector focus on the starter engine for economic growth—food production and availability, the input, processing and support industries, policies that stimulate development, and infrastructure that supports development. Some of the money and food is spent in market towns and urban centers (input and processing agribusiness, credit institutions, policy setting, research and educational institutions, and food aid.)

Another issue is relative allocations to competing countries. It is clear that some countries have less development promise and that in others a given investment will likely yield more in income growth, growth in food consumption, benefit to the natural resources, and advancement in international trading status. Country allocations should be heavily influenced by these factors.

Resource limits dictate that USAID organize and do business in a way that makes most effective use of those resources and the talented men and women they provide.

There is another very important personnel issue. The perception is strongly held, both internally and externally, that there is far too much dependence by USAID on external contractors for expertise, gathering and collating data for management, designing strategies, and recommending priorities.

Either the expertise is lacking, is too busy with process, or doesn't have the confidence, continuity, and management structure to effectively carry out these tasks.

Personnel

An agency-wide study of USAID's food and agriculture personnel, financed by the Asia/Near East bureau, analyzed the training, experience, promotion rate, and other key factors of about 300 agriculture, natural resources, rural development, and Food-for-Peace employees (about 265 were foreign service, 25 were civil service, and 10 were administratively determined appointments or staff on loan from universities). The study showed that

- There is an experience gap in the upper mid-level ranks. Sixty-nine percent of agriculture officers, for example, have 10 or fewer years of experience at USAID; 25% can or will retire in the next 5 years.
- The proportion of these four professional categories of backstops to total USAID professionals hasn't changed much during the 1980s.
- Recruitment has been driven by replacement of those departing rather than by future needs.
- Though promotion rates of agricultural officers below the senior foreign service level are comparable to those for other categories, promotion of these and other technical specialists into the senior foreign service has been at a lower rate. Beyond that, the perception is that management responsibilities held by agricultural officers, especially in larger missions, "are not given the proper amount of weight when assessed for impact against mission colleagues in other career fields, especially program and project development."
- Agricultural officers may be "viewed as stereotypes with specialized backgrounds and narrow focus" and this "could impact on the assessment—in the competitive promotion process."

It is relevant to note that agriculture and related staff, and the handling of agriculture and related matters—policy, technology, Food for Peace, project review, etc.,—are dispersed throughout USAID, and that employees in agriculture, rural development, and natural resources personnel categories are concentrated in Technical Resources (Development Resources in Latin America/Caribbean Bureau), and the Science and Technology Bureau (S&T). There are 15 Food-for-Peace personnel in the Food and Voluntary Assistance Bureau (FVA).

It is also noted that very few persons in these categories are in a position of office director or above, and that five of the last seven persons named to the top related nonpolitical appointment positions (Agency Director for Food and Agriculture, Human Resources, and Energy/Natural Resources) were not promotions from within. Though three members of the Food and Agriculture Task Force, largely DAAs chosen because of their senior positions and broad responsibilities in USAID, have had intensive experiences with Food for Peace, none of the members have come from any of the related, subject-matter personnel categories.

Because there is no agency-wide organizational focus for food and agriculture, there is no visible advancement cone that readily accepts and utilizes the combination of management skills and sector perspective that develops in capable professionals.

The report mentioned above noted that "without the recognition of critical management accomplishments and(or) training to broaden their skill base, specialists will continue to move to generalist areas in their quest for promotions and greater recognition and rewards."

Career advancement potential and willingness to stay with USAID certainly affect the quality, maturity and seniority of professionals.

Another issue here is the perspective brought to agency decisions and, therefore, the factors that may be considered in decisions. Perspective can be limited by the predominance of subject matter disciplines or orientation among senior staff and decision-makers.

There may be a parallel in the U.S. private sector. In the 1960s, management experts noted that people with master's degrees in business administration and those who were generalists helped companies succeed. More were needed in private industry to focus on long-term financial and management strategy, weigh competitive investment opportunities, and take tax and other laws into account to maximize return on investment. During the 1970s, these people had a seller's market.

Today, management experts say the best run companies generally have people in the top spots who know their products, who have come out of sales or technology. Perhaps the pendulum swung too far.

These two issues—balance and breadth of input to management decisions and perceived opportunity of technical people to impact decisions and to be promoted—are critical to personnel strength at USAID.

WORKING RELATIONSHIPS WITH U.S. AGRICULTURE AND NATURAL RESOURCES INTERESTS

To best advance the mutual interests of the U.S. and LDCs, USAID must have an open and constructive relationship with U.S. interest groups. This is especially important in the case of U.S. agriculture, because food and agriculture are so critical to LDC development, and because U.S. agriculture sorely needs expanded export markets.

A parallel need exists in relationships with U.S. environmental and natural resources interests. U.S. citizens have a high level of sensitivity and concern for the world's environment and stability of the natural resources. They recognize the fragility of the natural resources, especially in most LDCs, and the intense population pressure on these resources.

They are willing to invest time, attention, and money to help ensure that development efforts foster sustained development, prudently using the natural resources for the current generation, but also preserving and enhancing them for use by succeeding generations.

It is appropriate to review some of the interests of U.S. agriculture and how they mesh with USAID's interests and goals:

• Grain and soybean producers and handlers want larger export volume in the near term, then in the long term.
• Livestock and poultry groups want to export breeding stock semen, embryos, or day-old chicks.
• Processors and baggers want a high proportion of exports to be "value-added."

USAID cannot, of course, fully rationalize differing interests and goals of various groups.

It is significant that individual commodity groups are more concerned about their share of food aid and specific LDC competition with their commodity whereas the aggregate agricultural community would be more concerned about the total agricultural export volume. The aggregate community should also show relatively more interest in the long-term volume.

In addition to goals of increased income and consumption, and status of the natural resource base, USAID's interests are more long-term, with clear emphasis on sustainability.

The interests are generally mutual, but the mutuality is not always apparent. Financial stress in U.S. agriculture and some individual commodity anecdotes in the early 1980s suggested sharply conflicting interests.

Even specific, apparent conflicts are usually not complete or universal. For example, U.S. food processors' interests in value-added food aid conflicts with USAID's general objective to move the most calories at the lowest cost—raw grain. But many food aid programs, such as for schools or maternal/child health clinics, prescribe cereal/dried skim milk blends, and reports of nutrient deficiencies appearing among long- time residents of refugee camps dictate attention to fortifying emergency rations.

Because agricultural commodity group support for food aid is a good base for expanded interest in and support to all development programs, it is important that regard for USAID's management of food aid programs by these groups be high. FVA has worked hard to insure a stronger role by the regional bureaus, that proposals be complete and well documented, that most proposals be presented and approved well before the beginning of the fiscal year and to maintain good communication with commodity groups and contractors.

71

RECOMMENDATIONS

Two premises are self evident: (1) USAID's structure, staffing, procedures, and behavior should serve its mission and help achieve its goals and (2) staff satisfaction and morale are highest when that occurs.

Recommendations pertain to those items where it is perceived that improvements are needed and changes can be implemented. Recommendations marked with an asterisk (*) have been approved by Administrator Alan Woods.

General Program and Organization

1.* The food and agriculture goals, directions, and operational areas of investment as outlined in this document should be articulated in both internal and external documents, used as a basis for orientation and training of staff, and used as guidance in program design, implementation, and evaluation.

2. USAID should establish a single, central unit for food and agriculture, to provide coordinated leadership and support focus for the sector and also a personnel advancement cone for professionals.

    This unit should have sufficient budget for food and agriculture functions of (a) policy, planning, and strategy; (b) liaison and coordination with other development donors and lenders, including goals, directions, operational areas for investment and food aid; (c) project classification and databank; (d) science and technical support projects; (e) liaison with the international agricultural research centers; (f) liaison with U.S. agricultural and natural resource interest groups; (g) liaison with the Board for International Food and Agricultural Development and with nutrition, food, agriculture, and natural resources units of universities; (h) liaison with USDA and the Development Coordinating Committee's subcommittee on food aid; (i) coordination of USAID involvement in the Agricultural Trade and Development Mission program; (j) support to any interbureau food and agriculture sector groups or councils; (k) liaison with the personnel office and regional bureaus to achieve maximum education and experience for technical staff, and (l) support to private enterprise functions as well as efforts of the Trade and Development Program and OPIC.

    The recommendation includes the provision that appropriate technical staff for the geographic management function be budgeted and administered, as is now the case, in regional bureaus, but that they also be considered "members of the staff" or "courtesy staff members" of the central unit for the purpose of ensuring full weight of input to and coordination of the agency-wide subject matter functions. Regional bureaus and missions should retain budgets and responsibility for in-country projects, regional consulting support, and buy-ins to central support projects.

    This structure may accommodate the functions now performed by related sector councils. Should continuation of sector councils be deemed appropriate, there should be a single council with membership assuring representation and communication among both bureaus and disciplines, including nutrition. Recognizing that interbureau attention to individual subject areas is needed, such as the natural resources, nutrition, or other, special or ad hoc groups can and should be formed as needed to review projects or coordinate activities.

    This recommendation, in addition to rationale implied by functions outlined above, is based on two principles for an organization with responsibility for delivering either services or products over a wide geographic area: (1) A strong geographic management structure is essential to accommodate the unique needs of each target area. (2) A strong subject matter or product oriented management structure is essential to provide leadership in service or product development, research, quality control, and supporting the service or product in the field. It also must relate the service or product to central management, cooperators, funders, and the public.

    USAID has a strong geographic structure; it does not have a strong subject matter or product (food and agriculture program) structure.

3.* USAID should bring personnel at all decision-making and budget allocation levels to the point that they fully recognize and consider food aid a development resource paralleling DA or ESF in value. This calls for equivalent coverage in budget planning documents, abandoning the current tendency to use food aid as a "fill in" to replace shortages of DA or ESF, rewarding USAID officers who excel, and providing program management staff in accord with the dollar volume and physical volume of food aid. On a relative basis within USAID, the food aid function is now understaffed.

4. In cooperation with the U.S. Department of Agriculture (USDA), USAID should identify those LDCs with highest odds and potential for following the 23 advancing LDCs that increased imports of agricultural commodities in the 1970s, and identify priority areas for USAID effort—both food aid and agricultural development programs—in those identified countries. This is an important issue for the regional bureaus, mission directors, and agricultural development officers, and for the outside program panel mentioned in 19.

Because progress in those identified countries will certainly involve increased agricultural production and efficiency, USAID should work with USDA, other research entities, and U.S. industry groups to assess that production potential—acreage of good soil, water, and other resources—relative to consumption potential, and the nature and degree of competition with and benefit to U.S. agriculture that might be anticipated.

5.* USAID should continue constructive and productive participation in and follow-through to the agricultural trade and development missions handled in cooperation with USDA and the U.S. Department of State (USDS).

6. In missions, those food aid functions that relate to agriculture and rural development be either consolidated with agriculture and rural development in a single office, perhaps identified as Food and Agriculture, or that there be specific provisions for mutual involvement by food aid, agriculture, nutrition, and natural resources staff in planning development use of food aid, for coordination of related programs and policy efforts, and for utilization of generated local currency.

7. In AID/W, the Food-for-Peace regional divisions should be linked in some way with the agricultural, nutrition, rural development, and natural resources divisions of each regional bureau, perhaps incorporated in a food-and-agriculture office in the regional bureaus. This could help simplify and make consistent mission communication with AID/W and would help provide for parallel handling of the development features of food aid projects and those financed by DA or ESF. The budget responsibilities of a regional bureau Development Planning (DP) office are recognized, and these would remain with DP, as is true for DA and ESF.

8. Within the science and technology area, whether or not Recommendation 2 is implemented, agriculture, rural development, nutrition, and natural resources should be part of a single organizational unit, with appropriate sub-units. This single unit could be headed by a DAA or Agency Director. This would ease communication with regional bureaus and missions, diminish risk of functional or project overlap, and reduce administrative layers.

9. The significant work of PVOs as implementors of U.S. food aid programs and managers of important agricultural development programs should be linked by USAID with the food and agriculture offices of the missions and AID/W. The structure of this linkage should be developed.

10.* USAID should utilize some existing industry group or groups, such as the Agricultural Policy Advisory Committee established by Congress, to advise the Office of the U.S. Trade Representative and USDA on formulation of agricultural trade policy or groups that may form for other purposes, as two-way communication links between USAID and agricultural leaders.

USAID should similarly utilize existing environmental and natural resources interest groups as two-way communication links between USAID and interest group leaders.

Through such groups USAID can receive input to make programs most effective and can inform leaders about goals, directions, and impacts.

11. The international agricultural research centers should receive continued strong agency support. These centers are worldwide and multilaterally financed, relatively protected from external pressures that would dilute or divert resources, and sufficiently focused to allow substantive and continuing contribution to LDC needs.

Though there is still worldwide need for more calories, hence continued emphasis on and investment in basic food crops research, there should be increased investments in such centers as the International Service for National Agricultural Research (to strengthen LDC research and extension institutions) and the Asian Vegetable Research and Development Center to help accommodate the needs of advancing LDCs and the food and agriculture program directions listed earlier.

USAID should more fully utilize scientific liaisons and judgements from regional bureaus and missions in its input to the priorities and program directions of these centers. To ensure that USAID staff are continually in tune with this system, liaisons to the centers should provide appropriate mission and AID/W staff with timely information on U.S. investments in the center programs and on center priorities, accomplishments, and program changes. Liaisons to the centers should also encourage the centers' staffs to communicate and work closely with in-country USAID staff wherever possible.

Food Aid

12. USAID should determine the appropriate volume of food aid that should be sought for economic development (and emergency/disaster) purposes, consistent with development principles and experience, and that can be realistically administered under current law and policies. It should also determine what changes in U.S. laws, policies, or staffing would be needed to accommodate such use, with increased relative emphasis on achieving and measuring impact.

This recommendation in no way contradicts, and in fact supports, the important market development and other functions of food aid.

13.* USAID's administrator should meet at an early opportunity with the Secretary of Agriculture and counterpart members of the Development Coordinating Committee. The committee should charge its Food Aid Subcommittee to:

- Develop guidelines to be followed by the subordinate working group(s) for food aid allocation criteria, categories of use, and other factors that will encourage and make it easier for the agencies to achieve maximum development impact from food aid. These guidelines should include approval of food aid proposals 60 days before the beginning of the fiscal year.
- Ensure that working group designees by each agency be senior staff who support the multiple functions prescribed for food aid, and that each member actively function on a continuing basis, not routinely assigning the working group function to subordinate staff.
- Define the coordination and guidance role of the working group(s).
- Outline the roles of USDA and USAID in administering the several programs, clarifying that administration, including communication with field staff, is the role of the two administering agencies.
- Share with all related publics—commodity groups, shippers, PVOs, and others— the guidelines, roles, and modes of operation.

Beyond these general but very important issues, it is recommended that the working group(s) meet at least once and preferably twice each year in a developing country to review as a group on-going food aid programs and their development impacts, and to discuss with host country, USDA, and USAID personnel issues related to management and operations of the programs.

This recommendation acknowledges that there are necessary macro- budget and policy coordination roles (in contrast to the administering role) played by all agencies that are members of the Development Coordinating Committee and working group(s).

14.* USAID should continue to handle food aid proposals with sufficient dispatch, consistency, professionalism, and open communication that commodity groups, contractors, and other involved agencies would volunteer, "We may disagree on proposals or the final decision, but A.I.D. is always well prepared, proposals are well presented and documented, communication is complete, and the Agency behavior is as consistent and predictable as could be expected, considering its responsibilities and relationships with recipient countries. We rarely get surprised."

15. USAID should seek refinement of Public Law 480 legislation to simplify and articulate in a more clear manner the continuum of food aid programs supported by the American public for humanitarian, economic development, market development, and other functions.

Mission and AID/W Operations

16.* USAID food and agriculture staff, both in missions and in AID/W, should be aggressive in their communications and cooperation— perhaps meet regularly— with other donors, with multilateral lending agencies, and with other U.S. economic development efforts. Especially in-country, this is more possible and desirable because of continuing mission presence.

17. Mission agriculture staff should be involved and carry some responsibility for initiation, support, and coordination of USAID's private enterprise efforts and the work of the Trade and Development program and OPIC, which are so complementary to the agricultural development function.

18.* Guidance to new mission office heads and directors should emphasize that program continuity and persistence toward established, reachable objectives is expected and merits high marks in personnel evaluation. Such guidance would complement a 1985 cable to mission directors. It should be institutionalized in documents and be well known throughout USAID. Such guidance is needed, not only because program continuity is essential for maximum project impact toward goals, but also because of both pressures and temptations to respond to "the latest that is in favor," and because of both internal and external perceptions that high motivation exists in these positions to put each leader's "stamp" on a mission program by replacing an inordinate number of projects.

The recommendation is not intended to inhibit needed change.

19. Missions (in some cases, subregion mission groups) should consider establishing an outside program panel (external to the mission but including some USAID people with in-country experience and perhaps host and private sector country people) to provide guidance and continuity to food and agriculture programs. Membership could be for a term of years, but with some rotation, and would include people who have close familiarity with and dedication to that country's development.

Because USAID operations generally provide 3-year to 4-year personnel rotations, many to other regions, such assistance could aid continuity, assure program direction response as a country advances, and help provide, through USAID members, an institutional history of program impact.

This would also allow more complete utilization of USAID staff who have long term familiarity with given countries. It could also add strength and credibility to assessments of agricultural development potential and judgement regarding country resource allocation.

20.* The practice should be established that for most mission, regional, or agency food and agricultural sector program review teams, USAID staff select and include at least one person who is an elected or employed officer of a national or major state agricultural or natural resources group, a private sector subject matter specialist, a state agriculture or natural resources commissioner, or a state or area extension specialist.

21.* There should be increased communication with contractors, by both mission and AID/W personnel, to insure that contractor staff are aware of mission/agency policies, directions, priorities, and handling of problems. In an LDC and in the United States this will enhance the feeling of mutual interest, ability to support the program, and presentation of a coherent posture.

Personnel

22. USAID criteria and guidelines on promotion of technical staff to and within the Senior Foreign Service should be modified, and experience tracks be provided to allow a reasonable proportion of food and agriculture professionals to qualify for and be moved into senior ranks. In this process, a comparison with guidelines for technical people in other federal units guided by the same law— USDS, USDA (both the Foreign Agricultural Service and the Animal and Plant Health Inspection Service), U.S. Department of Commerce, and United States Information Service— would be appropriate.

23. Personnel classification backstops in agriculture, rural development, natural resources, and nutrition should be combined and increased emphasis should be placed on the subject matter qualifications at the time of employment and in continuing education of staff. This would be consistent with USAID's decision to not hire new staff in the food aid backstop but to provide a "certification level" of training for persons of any backstop who have significant food aid responsibilities.

There are now relatively few persons in the nutrition backstop. Consolidation of the other three has been recommended by others in order to provide more assignment flexibility and promotional opportunity for personnel.

USAID should recruit new professional staff within these backstops to meet future needs. It sorely needs persons educated and experienced in input agribusinesses, aquaculture, horticulture, animal agriculture, food processing, and international agricultural trade. USAID must accumulate the skills and talents needed for the food and agriculture programs' goals and directions.

To help meet the latter need, USAID should also provide more long- term and short-term education of current staff, including graduate study, detached service assignments in international centers and universities; and experience in policy analysis, agricultural business, natural resources, food processing, and international trade. This would be beyond current long-term training practices, would specifically take into account that 21 staff in the four backstops (7%) are on complement this fiscal year. Reducing numbers on complement could allow increasing, at any given time, the number gaining needed education and experience.

Operating Effectiveness

24. Travel funds available for scientific and technical support personnel should be sharply increased, to allow increased technical support to missions, monitoring of contractors, and relating to clientele groups. The increase recommended is from a currently financed travel of about 15 days international and 6 days domestic total per fiscal year to a level that would provide transportation and per diem for 56 days (40 working days and 16 weekend travel days) of international travel (2 weeks per quarter) and 10 days of domestic travel per year.

At present, travel funds and policy limit S&T's and regional bureau's support value to missions, contribute to perceptions (and perhaps reality) that research and technical support priorities are not responsive to mission and regional bureaus needs. Fund shortages and policies necessitate missions using outside consultants and by-passing often-preferred USAID help (and miss giving these people the

76

acquaintance with mission programs they ought to have) because operating expense funds are limited and program funds can be used only for outside consultants. They also limit staff contact with leading scientists and thinkers in their disciplines, domestic and university contractors, and U.S. industry and interest groups.

This recommendation applies to technical people in regional bureaus, in S&T, and in missions, whose expertise may be needed for project-related work in other missions.

To achieve this, increased appropriations may not be needed. The solution may lie in removing Congressional constraints on using mission program money to bring AID/ W staff to the country, changes in USAID policy or allocations, or even reducing personnel to free money for travel.

Where the money is available is a second issue. A significant portion in the missions would insure travel most responsive to mission needs.

25. Every professional work station should be equipped with a computer that has direct linkages to mission and AID/W personnel for transmittal of data, correspondence, queries, and messages; a phone with message recording device; and convenient access to copying and telefaxing equipment.

Each professional work group should have secretarial support for the receptionist, meeting arrangement, and other support functions.

USAID's phone book and directory should list the office, telefax, and home phone numbers of each employee.

Communication with External Groups

26.* USAID should designate one staff member and one alternate to maintain regular communication with officers of each key U.S. agricultural commodity group, such as the U.S. Corn Growers, Wheat Growers, U.S. Feed Grains Council, Florida Citrus Commission, and National Cattlemen's Association, comparable to existing communication links with the American Soybean Association.

Communication areas would include related development projects, food aid, work at international research centers, advances by LDC national research systems, LDC production trends, LDC sources of genetic materials, and LDC income and food consumption trends.

27.* USAID should continue to allocate a significant proportion of Biden-Pell development education funds to agricultural and related food, agribusiness, and natural resources audiences. (A total of $2.5 to $3 million has been available in each of recent fiscal years.)

28.* USAID, through mission staff and contractors, should annually publish a limited number of project reports or fact sheets that document the extent to which programs in food and agriculture have directly or indirectly contributed to the goals of increased income, food consumption, and status of the natural resource base, and evidence of resultant benefit accruing to the United States.

29.* USAID should arrange 40 speeches per year to national, regional, and major state groups on the above topics, five or more to be given by the administrator and 10 or more by assistant administrators and DAAs, to inform the groups of programs and relationships and to allow top USAID officers to receive feedback and maintain sensitivity to mutual U.S. and LDC interests.